fall 2021

Mission

The *Community Literacy Journal* is an interdisciplinary journal that publishes both scholarly work that contributes to theories, methodologies, and research agendas and work by literacy workers, practitioners, and community literacy program staff. We are especially committed to presenting work done in collaboration between academics and community members, organizers, activists, teachers, and artists.

We understand "community literacy" as including multiple domains for literacy work extending beyond mainstream educational and work institutions. It can be found in programs devoted to adult education, early childhood education, reading initiatives, or work with marginalized populations. It can also be found in more informal, ad hoc projects, including creative writing, graffiti art, protest songwriting, and social media campaigns.

For us, literacy is defined as the realm where attention is paid not just to content or to knowledge but to the symbolic means by which it is represented and used. Thus, literacy makes reference not just to letters and to text but to other multimodal, technological, and embodied representations, as well. Community literacy is interdisciplinary and intersectional in nature, drawing from rhetoric and composition, communication, literacy studies, English studies, gender studies, race and ethnic studies, environmental studies, critical theory, linguistics, cultural studies, education, and more.

Subscriptions

Donations to the *CLJ* in any amount can be made with a check made out to "FIU English Department," with *Community Literacy Journal* in the memo line.

Send to:

>Paul Feigenbaum
>Department of English
>Florida International University
>DM462D
>11200 SW 8th St.
>Miami, FL 33199

Donors at the $40 level or above will receive a courtesy print subscription of the academic year's issues.

Cover Artist and Art

Gabrielle Ricci IG @gabriellericciart

I'm an Afro-Latina artist from Columbus Ohio. I've been drawing, painting and crafting ever since I could remember. My favorite medium is digital art. I use my iPad to create art focused on natural hair and women of color. Afros, curls and kinks are all right up my alley. Drawing mermaids is one of my favorite things to do. Happy imagery and fun colors are my focus. I want people to see my art, feel happy and at the same time represented.

Submissions

Submissions for the articles section of the journal should clearly demonstrate engagement with community literacy scholarship, particularly scholarship previously published in the Community Literacy Journal. The editors seek work that pushes the field forward in exciting and perhaps unexpected ways. Case studies, qualitative and/ or quantitative research, conceptual articles, etc., ranging from 20-25 manuscript pages, are welcome. If deemed appropriate, we will send the manuscript out to readers for blind review. You can expect a report in 10-12 weeks.

The CLJ also welcomes shorter manuscripts (8-12 pages) for two new sections: **Community Literacy Project and Program Profiles** will discuss innovative and impactful community-based projects and programs that are grounded in best practices. We encourage community-based practitioners and non-profit staff to submit for this section. Profiles should draw on community literacy scholarship, but they are not expected to have the extended lit reviews that are customary in the articles section of the journal. If you are a community member wanting to submit, and it is your first time writing for an academic journal, we are happy to offer mentorship and answer questions. Pieces co-authored by multiple stakeholders in a project are also welcome.

Please submit using our online submission system. Contact the Project and Program Profiles Editor, Vincent Portillo, with questions at vportill@syr.edu.

Issues in Community Literacy will offer targeted analysis, reflection, and/or complication of ongoing challenges associated with the work of community literacy. Potential subjects for this section include (but are not limited to): building/sustaining infrastructure, navigating institutional constraints, pursuing community literacy in graduate school, working with vulnerable populations, building ethical relationships, realizing reciprocity, and negotiating conflicts among partners. We imagine this as a space for practitioners to raise critical issues or offer a response to an issue raised in a previous volume of the CLJ.

We encourage community-based practitioners and non-profit staff to submit for this section. If you are a community member wanting to submit, and it is your first time writing for an academic journal, we are happy to offer mentorship and answer questions. Pieces co-authored by multiple stakeholders in a project are also welcome.

Please submit using our online submission system. Contact the Issues in Community Literacy Editor, Cayce Wicks, with questions at cwick003@fiu.edu.

Coda: Community Writing and Creative Work welcomes submissions of poetry, creative nonfiction, short stories, and multigenre work on any topics that have ensued from community writing projects. This may be work about community writing projects, and this may be expressed in ways we have yet to imagine. We ask authors to include a personal reflection about the submission itself—information about your community writing group (if you belong to one); your personal journey as a writer; what inspired you to write your piece; and anything else you'd care to share about your life—as an invitation for the author and Coda's readers to consider writing and activism as intertwined.

Please submit using our online submission system. Contact the Coda Editorial Collective at coda.editors@gmail.com.

Advertising

Community Literacy Journal welcomes advertising. The journal is published twice annually, in the Fall and Spring (November and May). Deadlines for advertising are two months prior to publication (September and March).

Ad Sizes and Pricing

Half page (trim size 5.5X4.25): $200
Full page (trim size 5.5X8.5): $350
Inside back cover (trim size 5.5X8.5): $500
Inside front cover (trim size 5.5X8.5): $600

Format

We accept .PDF, .JPG, .TIF or .EPS. All advertising images should be camera-ready and have a resolution of 300 dpi. For more information, please contact Veronica House (housev@colorado.edu) and Paul Feigenbaum (pfeigenb@fiu.edu).

Copyright © 2021 *Community Literacy Journal*
ISSN 1555-9734

Community Literacy Journal is a member of the Council of Editors of Learned Journals.

Production and distribution managed by Parlor Press.

Publication of the *Community Literacy Journal* is made possible through the generous support of the English Department and the Writing and Rhetoric Program at Florida International University. The *CLJ* is a journal of the Coalition for Community Writing. Current issues and archives are available open access at https://digitalcommons.fiu.edu/communityliteracy/

Editorial Board

Jonathan Alexander, *University of California Irvine*
Steven Alvarez, *St. John's University*
April Baker Bell, *Michigan State University*
Kirk Branch, *Montana State University*
Stephanie Briggs, *Be.Still.Move.*
Laurie Cella, *Shippensburg University*
David Coogan, *Virginia Commonwealth University*
Ellen Cushman, *Northeastern University*
Lisa Dush, *DePaul University*
Jenn Fishman, *Marquette University*
Linda Flower, *Carnegie Mellon University*
Beth Godbee, *Heart-Head-Hands.com*
Eli Goldblatt, *Temple University, Emeritus*
Laurie Grobman, *Pennsylvania State University Berks*
Shirley Brice Heath, *Stanford University*
Glenn Hutchinson, *Florida International University*
Tobi Jacobi, *Colorado State University*
Ben Kuebrich, *West Chester University*
Carmen Kynard, *Texas Christian University*
Paula Mathieu, *Boston College*
Seán Ronan McCarthy, *James Madison University*
Michael Moore, *DePaul University*
Beverly Moss, *The Ohio State University*
Steve Parks, *The University of Virginia*
Jessica Pauszek, *Boston College*
Eric Darnell Pritchard, *University of Arkansas Fayetteville*
Jessica Restaino, *Montclair State University*
Elaine Richardson, *The Ohio State University*
Lauren Rosenberg, *University of Texas at El Paso*
Tiffany Rousculp, *Salt Lake Community College*
Iris Ruiz, *University of California Merced*
Donnie Sackey, *University of Texas at Austin*
Rachael W. Shah, *University of Nebraska-Lincoln*
Erec Smith, *York College of Pennsylvania*
John Trimbur, *Emerson College*
Stephanie Wade, *Searsport District High School, Maine*
John Warnock, *University of Arizona*
Christopher Wilkey, *Northern Kentucky University*

COMMUNITY LITERACY Journal

Editors	Paul Feigenbaum, *Florida International University* Veronica House, *University of Denver*
Senior Assistant Editor and Issues in Community Literacy Editor	Cayce Wicks, *Florida International University*
Journal Manager	Erin Daugherty, *University of Arkansas at Fayetteville*
Book and New Media Review Editor	Jessica Shumake, *University of Notre Dame*
Consulting Editor and Project Profiles Editor	Vincent Portillo, *Boston College*
Coda: Community Writing and Creative Work Editorial Collective	Kefaya Diab, *Loyola University Maryland* Leah Falk, *Rutgers University, Camden* Chad Seader, *William Penn University* Alison Turner, *Independent Scholar, Denver* Kate Vieira, *University of Wisconsin, Madison* Stephanie Wade, *Searsport District High School, Maine*
Senior Copyeditor	Elvira Carrizal-Dukes, *University of Texas at El Paso*
Copyeditors	Quiana Cutts, *Mississippi State University* Adam Hubrig, *Sam Houston State University* Charisse Iglesias, *University of Arizona* Walter Lucken IV, *Wayne State University* Kelly Whitney, *The Ohio State University*

community literacy journal

COMMUNITY LITERACY *journal*

Fall 2021
Volume 16, Issue 1

Guest Editor: Elaine Richardson

Editor's Introduction

1   *Critical Social Justice Possibilities in Hiphop Literacies: An Introduction*
    Elaine Richardson with Steve Lessner

Articles

10 *'She Ugly': Black Girls, Women in Hiphop and Activism—Hiphop Feminist Literacies Perspectives*
    Elaine Richardson aka Dr. E

32 *Higher Hussle: Nipsey's Post Hip Hop Literacies*
    Marquese McFerguson and Aisha Durham

45 *Free Your Mind and Your Practice Will Follow: Exploring Hip-Hop Habits of Mind as a Practice of Educational Freedom*
    Toby S. Jenkins

69 *"An Art of Truth in Things": Confronting Hiphop Illiteracies in Writing Classrooms at Predominantly White Colleges and Universities*
    Tessa Brown

Book and New Media Reviews

91 *From the Book and New Media Review Editor's Desk*
    Jessica Shumake, Editor

92 *Literacy as Conversation: Learning Networks in Urban and Rural Communities* by Eli Goldblatt and David A. Jolliffe
    Reviewed by Rachel E.H. Edwards

97 *Family Literacies: Shared Reading with Young Children* by Rachael Levy and Mel Hall
Reviewed by Megen Farrow Boyett

104 *Transnational Feminist Itineraries: Situating Theory and Activist Practice* edited by Ashwini Tambe and Millie Thayer
Reviewed by Curtis J. Jewell

111 *Words No Bars Can Hold: Literacy Learning in Prison* by Deborah Appleman
Reviewed by Walter Lucken IV

115 *Queer Literacies: Discourses and Discontents* by Mark McBeth
Reviewed by Mary F. McGinnis

120 *Literacy Heroines: Women and the Written Word* by Alice S. Horning
Reviewed by Andrea McCrary

PARLOR PRESS
EQUIPMENT FOR LIVING

Now with Parlor Press!

Studies in Rhetorics and Feminism
Series Editors: Cheryl Glenn and Shirley Wilson Logan

New Releases

Writing in the Clouds: Inventing and Composing in Internetworked Writing Spaces by John Logie

Writing Spaces: Readings on Writing Volume 4

Running, Thinking, Writing: Embodied Cognition in Composition by Jackie Hoermann-Elliott

English Studies Online: Programs, Practices, Possibilities, edited by William P. Banks and Susan Spangler

Feminist Circulations: Rhetorical Explorations across Space and Time, edited by Jessica Enoch, Danielle Griffin and Karen Nelson

MLA Mina Shaughnessy Prize and CCCC Best Book Award 2021!

Creole Composition: Academic Writing and Rhetoric in the Anglophone Caribbean, edited by Vivette Milson-Whyte, Raymond Oenbring, and Brianne Jaquette

Check Out Our New Website!

Discounts, blog, open access titles, instant downloads, and more.

www.parlorpress.com

CLJ **Discount:** Use CLJ20 at checkout to receive a 20% discount on all titles not on sale through February 1, 2022.

Critical Social Justice Possibilities in Hiphop Literacies: An Introduction

Elaine Richardson with Steve Lessner

Hiphop manifested during the Black Power Era. Black Studies scholars assert that Hiphop pedagogy is useful when locating Black diaspora movement for liberation (Saucier &Woods). Hiphop is inextricably bound to Black Lives Matter (BLM) era of the freedom struggle. The Black Lives Matter Hiphop generation is shaping freedom in their own terms, sounds, and likeness (Cohen). Begun by Alicia Garza, Opal Tometi and Patrisse Khan Cullors in 2013 as a hashtag after the vigilante murder of Trayvon Martin, these loving and powerful Black queer women started a movement, emphasizing the sanctity of all Black life, prioritizing the most marginalized ones. The global Black Lives Matter (BLM) movement provides synergy for Hiphop [and others] to develop coherent political frameworks to demand long overdue justice.

However, some artists such as Kanye West, Lil Wayne, Waka Flocka Flame, 50 Cent, and others, appeared to be going down on the wrong side of history in their support of Donald Trump in the 2020 Presidential campaign. These rappers backed Trump, despite his support of white supremacist groups, confederate monuments, police brutality, anti-Black Lives Matter tactics, failures around Covid-19, which cost disproportionate loss of Black and Brown lives, and backlash against the first Black president-Barack Obama. (McGrady) Hiphop and Trump make for strange bedfellows. We see these artists as wasting their clout on Trump. Barack Obama called upon Jay-Z to support his campaign and the rest is history. Speaking to CNN political analyst, Michael Smerconish, about Kanye West's support of Trump, Meek Mill expresses shock and disappointment:

> ...Kanye came out of nowhere and just went red hat, and that was kind of against everything we represent. I don't know what he represents, but coming up in the Hiphop community, we came up fighting, and fighting for our rights for a long time, and what that red hat represents don't really represent what we've been fighting for our whole lives. (https://www.cnn.com/videos/tv/2018/12/01/meek-mill-on-prison-reform-kanye-new-album.cnn)

Whether some members of the Hiphop community are misguided or only focused on their own individual success, at the same time, the Black Lives Matter Hiphop generation is striving for collective progress. In response to Derek Chauvin's very public horrific nonchalant knee-to-the-neck murder of George Floyd, that went viral, a renaissance in Black art for social justice re-emerged alongside protests across the nation and the world. Amanda Gorman, in a discussion with Michelle Obama, emphasizes that the renaissance in Black art, in fashion, music, dance, visual arts, and all forms of human expression, is historical, grounded in the Black experience and inextricably linked to Black Lives Matter becoming the largest social movement.

With regard to visual arts, producer, entrepreneur and one of the founders of Verzuz, Kasseem Dean aka Swiss Beats is working to disrupt the art world. He has been pushing the millionaires and billionaires of the Hiphop generation to own the culture rather than only creating it. Swiss is a graduate of the Harvard Business School and sits on the Boards of art museums and galleries in the U.S. and in London. Along with his wife, Alicia Keyes, Kanye West, Jay-Z and Beyonce, Sean Combs and others, he is a collector of Black art and seeks to cultivate the importance of collecting even among non-wealthy Black people. Swiss founded the "No Commission" Art Fair. In this space and others Swiss provides a venue for Black visual artists to exhibit and retain 100% of their sales. He is also organizing around the issue of royalties for visual artists as is the practice in 70 other countries throughout the world. If this change comes, Black artists will be able to profit for any resales of their work during their lifetime. As Yvonne Bynoe states, Swiss is among the new "generation of African-American art collectors and patrons [who] are shaking up the art world. They embody the ethos of Hip Hop culture: Succeeding in a world not designed for you by reconfiguring it." (https://www.blackartinamerica.com/index.php/2021/05/04/how-the-hip-hop-generation-is-disrupting-the-art-world/)

With regard to music, there will always be artists that bring a strong message. Roc Nation released an album of songs about revolution, police brutality, genocide, racism, and more on *Reprise,* with music by various artists such as Ambre, Rapsody, Vic Mensa, Ant Clemons, King Mel, Sebastian Kole and others. Tobe Nwigwe and his team dropped a short and powerful EP, *Pandemic Project,* showcasing ear and mind-opening Hiphop beats and rhymes such as "I Need You To" urging listeners to become familiar with the evidence surrounding the murders of Breonna Taylor and Elijah McCain and demand their killers be brought to justice. *Pandemic Project* is a Black empowerment EP featuring tunes such as "Make it Home," which is basically a prayer song for Black people to make it home alive. But if by chance in this white supremacist world we do not make it back to our hood, our nappy heads will make it to heaven, to our "nappy headed Christ." The overall message of "Fresh Air" is to guard one's soul, breathe, seek truth and one's best self. "Try Jesus" is a humorous critique of the Christian non-violent teaching, to turn the other cheek. In "Hip-hop Has Been Standing Up for Black Lives for Decades: 15 Songs and Why They Matter," Zaru and Brown survey songs from 1982-2020 that address Black experiences through memorable lyrics rooted in protest: dreams, suffering, rage, hunger, joy, survival, and unity.

In 2015, Janelle Monae released the protest song "Hell You Talmbout" with the Wondaland crew. The song admonishes listeners to say the names of Black people wrongfully killed by police and vigilantes. She performed the song in 2017 at the Women's March in Washington, DC. September 25, 2021 in collaboration with the African American Policy Forum Monae dropped another version, "#SayHerName (Hell You Talmbout)." This song features:

> Kimberlé Crenshaw, Beyoncé, Alicia Keys, Chlöe x Halle, Tierra Whack, Isis V., Zoë Kravitz, Brittany Howard, Asiahn, Mj Rodriguez, Jovian Zayne, An-

gela Rye, Nikole Hannah-Jones, Brittany Packnett Cunningham and Alicia Garza. Through this song, these women unite — not just as entertainers and activists, but also as daughters — and aim to share the stories of our sisters who have died at the hands of police. (https://tinyurl.com/yc2tue45)

Collaborations between activists and artists have a long and impactful history in the Black freedom struggle. Tamika Mallory is an organizer, activist, author, speaker. She has a long history of organizing, including the 2017 Women's March, which she co-led. She co-founded Until Freedom, an organization that fights racial injustice. Jeezy features Tamika Mallory on the song "Oh Lord." It is built around bluesy and soulful vocals from "Trouble So Hard" by Vera Hall collected by ethnomusicologist Alan Lomax in 1937. Those vocals are mixed in with parts of Tamika Mallory's May 29th, 2020 speech in Minneapolis as part of the nationwide protest around George Floyd's murder. Tamika's words express heart felt rage and an exacting analysis of the state of perpetual emergency experienced by the Black community. In his raspy signature tone, Jeezy is flowing with straight facts. The song is history, culture, education and protest all (w)rapped together.

Tamika Mallory did a guest appearance on the 2021 Grammy show with Lil Baby of the song "The Bigger Picture." Lil Baby is a platinum selling award winning rapper, known for being a voice of the streets. Among his many powerful words and stories, included in the song, one of my favorites is: "I can't lie like I don't rap about killing and dope/But I'm telling my youngins to vote/I did what I did cause I didn't have no choice or no hope." It's important that Lil Baby used his platform to showcase Tamika Mallory and her message to the multi-racial and 8.8 million viewers of the Grammy audience. She directed some of her words to President Joe Biden, demanding justice, equity, policy and spoke of the hell Black people have been catching for over 400 years. As equally important as hard-hitting words, Hiphop is all about fashion and style. In addition to her words and staged protest, Tamika's presentation was enhanced by the fly outfit she wore. In a conversation with Tamron Hall "Tamika Mallory Was Afraid That Her Grammys Performance Would Be Edited," Tamika discussed that she always partners with designers who have a commitment to the cause, such as Vietnamese designer, Cong Tri. There is power in unity.

Looking briefly at the Hiphop community performing other actions for social change, Meek Mill and Jay-Z partnered with New England Patriots' owner, Robert Kraft, Philadelphia 76ers' partner, Michael Rubin, Brooklyn Nets partner, Clara Wu Tsai among others to start REFORM Alliance. They appointed political commentator, Van Jones, as the organization's CEO. REFORM Alliance aims to halt the cycle of the criminal justice system that keeps people on parole and probation, for violations, such as popping wheelies on one's motor bike, or misdemeanor assault, and returning people to jail and in the system for extended terms. (France) This is what happened to Meek Mill, who has become somewhat of a poster case for prison reform. Meek Mill's release from prison is the result of #FreeMeekMill movement involving organizations such as the Color of Change, on the ground supporters, as well as celebrities and sports stars such as LeBron James, Questlove, T.I., Philadelphia Eagles players, Colin Kaepernick, and of course Jay-Z, who penned a *New York Times* Op-ed

"The Criminal Justice System Stalks Black People Like Meek Mill." In September of 2020, Mill and Jay-Z's organization have realized some change beyond Meek's release from prison. REFORM Alliance successfully advocated for California law to reduce probation: for misdemeanors one year, and two years for felonies. In January 2021, three bills were passed in Michigan. "Michigan had the sixth highest rate of probation supervision in the country. Now that Governor Gretchen Whitmer signed the bills into law, Michigan is on pace to decrease the state's overall caseloads by 8.4 percent." (Aniftos)

It is interesting to imagine possibilities for transformation if REFORM Alliance and Jay-Z linked their platform and resources to organizers such as Mariame Kaba and Ruthie Wilson Gilmore. In thinking about prison reform vs. prison abolition, Kaba asserts:

> While some offer calls for reform, such calls ignore the reality that an institution grounded in the commodification of human beings, through torture and the deprivation of their liberty, cannot be made good. The logic of using policing, punishment, and prison has not proven to address the systemic causes of violence. It is in this climate that we argue that abolition of the prison-industrial complex is the most moral political posture available to us. Because the deconstruction of the American system of mass incarceration is possible, and it is time. (25)

As Alicia Garza observes, it takes organized movement of those affected to create lasting social change:

> The real story behind any successful movement is many people coming together to create the change they want to see in the world. This truth has been obscured by popular narratives of successful social change that tend to revolve around the courageous actions and moral clarity of one person, usually a cisgender heterosexual man (212).

This seems to describe Ice Cube's approach with *A Contract with Black America* (CWBA) (contractwithblackamerica.us/wp-content/uploads/CWBA-Full-Contract.pdf). As Ice Cube explains, in an interview with journalist, Roland Martin, he set out to create a bi-partisan initiative to make whichever party that got into power (Democratic or Republican in the 2020 election) work to repair oppression of Blacks as a protected group. He developed the CWBA after the George Floyd killing and social protests and aimed to make concrete demands (Ice Cube Interview). The CWBA received criticism for omitting important entities of Black community (e. g. Black women, queer people, undocumented people, and more), and received negative evaluation from many for being seen as working with the Trump Administration. Though Ice Cube has since added a section on Black women, it is problematic to create a comprehensive document.

Roland Martin introduced Ice Cube to Alicia Garza during Cube's interview. Garza explained to him that his approach of going to the Trump Administration to make a transaction was misguided, and that it would be more productive if he shared his platform and joined forces with organizations such as hers (Black2theFuture.Org), to bring many thousands together in the power of organized movement. Hopefully, Garza and Cube get together.

There are countless examples of critical social justice work and possibilities underway in the Hiphop community, too many to name, as well as many that we are not aware of. Our aim is to shine light on the work that abounds in the midst of the twin pandemics by scholars, educators, activists and artists. Hiphop is the people. There's power in the people. Critical social justice possibilities in Hiphop literacies is about possibilities in people. As educators, we cannot best serve those we do not love. Love is critical. In that spirit, we proudly present the four articles that comprise this special issue.

Elaine Richardson's 'She Ugly': Black Girls, Women in Hiphop and Activism-Hiphop Feminist Literacies Perspectives" draws upon Hiphop feminism, studies of Black girlhood, and Black women and girls' literacies to illuminate the layered and violent narratives that shape society's treatment of Black women and girls, what these narratives look like in everyday life, how they are taken up and negotiated in different social spheres, such as an afterschool club for Black middle school girls and the platforms and artistry of women Hiphop artists and creatives. Richardson considers what activism is possible through juxtaposing Black girls as emerging creatives, celebrity corporate artist activists Nicki Minaj and Cardi B, independent activist artists such as Noname and dream hampton. Given the far-reaching representations of Black women and girls in popular culture, the art, lives and platforms of women in Hiphop are critical sites to understanding complexities, strategies and possibilities for social change.

In "Higher Hussle: Nipsey's Post Hip Hop Literacies," Marquese McFerguson and Aisha Durham offer an analysis of Nipsey Hussle and the critical social justice Hiphop literacies he performed, through the ways he stood against the white-owned mainstream music industry and the roles ascribed to Black men. Through owning his music, its production and distribution, building a business in his community and investing in its people, Hussle demonstrates an emancipated Blackness through economics, creative Black political empowerment, and literacy in the collective interest of Black people. Hussle imagined radical change from the bottom-up, drawing upon his Black diaspora identity (Eritrean and Los-Angeles), his other outlawed identity (as a former gang banger with insight into gang life as a mode of survival in the hood), and a successful self-made independent artist. McFerguson and Durham also show Nipsey's attunement to the interiority of Black masculinity, exposing the fullness of Black life, as his music and commentary drops the mask and rescripts the hardcore street Black male rapper, to expose structural conditions. In these ways Nipsey demonstrates a higher hussle.

Drawing from books written by Hiphop artists, Hiphop documentaries, song lyrics and interviews with Hiphop educators and scholars, Toby Jenkins distills nine Hiphop-centered values, beliefs, attitudes, and behaviors clustered around approach, drive, and posture, that educators must develop to be literate in contemporary global culture. In this article, entitled "Free Your Mind and Your Practice Will Follow: Exploring Hip-Hop Habits of Mind as a Practice of Educational Freedom," Jenkins argues that "The messages and deeper forms of understanding derived from the perspectives, actions, and behaviors of hip-hop community members can be seen as a social justice possibility because they build efficacy among communities that have been culturally miseducated." She contends that for far too long, Hiphop pedagogies have been seen as central to the success of Black and Brown students, when educators themselves must be centered in Hiphop as a professional mindset in their own lives. Jenkins asserts that a hip-hop mindset is beneficial to educators because it can also help them to explore possibilities, imagine new realities, and feel more free to bring all of who they culturally are into their professional practice. The "Hip-Hop mindset" is a way of thinking and being that can help bridge communities with the core outcome being collective responsibility for social justice.

Tessa Brown's "'The Art of Truth in Things': Confronting Hiphop Illiteracies in Writing Classrooms at Predominantly White Colleges and Universities" examines her research on Hiphop composition pedagogy at a predominantly white university. As a young queer white Jewish woman graduate student, striving to show up for social and racial justice, Brown's goal was to engage students in the global phenomenon of Hiphop, celebrate Black cultural practices, critically examine exploitation, misrepresentation and appropriation of Black culture and people, by corporate music conglomerates and American capitalism, expand students' writing identities, and prime them for transformation of their ideologies around anti-Blackness, with an eye toward social change. Brown used Hiphop songs, videos, and scholarship that engaged themes of literacy, discourse, the writing process, citation use, and Black Language with non-Hiphop texts from writing studies. Her collaborating researcher focused more on Hiphop culture, rappers as writers, thinkers, and rhetors, highlighting their lyrics, sonic tapestry, visuals, and context. Combined they taught 4 courses centered in Hiphop composition pedagogy, in which students wrote essays, research papers, did close readings, and in Brown's course, wrote literacy narratives.

Through student exit interviews, Brown found that her course design did not provide opportunities for her students to reflect on their own raced and gendered identities, producing a colorblind classroom environment, which for the most part, left students inadequately positioned to significantly discuss the very topics she hoped they would critically process: anti-Blackness, systemic racism, and Black cultural resilience, resistance, compliance, and critical negotiation of the American systems of racism, sexism, capitalism and empire. From her students of color, she learned that the course seemed more geared toward helping white students develop a critical lens for understanding their consumption of a steady diet of stereotypes of commodified Hiphop AND rappers' resistance and resilience. Further, she found that students needed critical sociolinguistic grounding in Black and Hiphop language to truly appreciate Hiphop. Brown asserts that Hiphop composition pedagogy must be anchored in reflexivity, that allows students to locate themselves with regard to power, to promote collective solidarity building, and not individual achievement.

Dr. E would like to thank the CLJ Editors Veronica and Paul for their patience and support through the process of putting this special issue together. Thanks also go out to the reviewers Crystal Endsley, Beth Godbee, Lauren Leigh Kelly, Steve Lessner,

Heidi Lewis, Gwendolyn Pough, and Qiana Cutts. Copyeditor: Dr. Qiana M. Cutts, Assistant Professor, Department of Counseling, Educational Psychology and Foundations, Mississippi State University. qmc24@msstate.edu.

Works Cited

Aniftos, Rania. "Michigan Passes Prison Reform Laws Supported by Meek Mill & Jay-Z's REFORM Alliance," *Billboard Magazine*. Billboard.com. January 4, 2021. Accessed November 24, 2021. https://www.billboard.com/music/rb-hip-hop/michigan-prison-reform-laws-meek-mill-jay-z-reform-alliance-9506880/

Bynoe, Yvonne. "How the Hip Hop Generation is Disrupting the Art World," BlackArtInAmerica.com *Black Art In America*. Accessed November 22, 2021.https://www.blackartinamerica.com/index.php/2021/05/04/how-the-hip-hop-generation-is-disrupting-the-art-world/

Cohen, Cathy J. "Afterword: When Will Black Lives Matter: Neoliberalism, Democracy, and the Queering of American Activism in the Post-Obama Era," Nielson, Erik, and Travis L. Gosa, editors. *The Hip Hop & Obama Reader*. Oxford University Press, 2015. pp. 280-290.

Cube, Ice. *The Contract with Black America*. Written with Introduction by Darrick Hamilton, and input from other experts. https://contractwithblackamerica.us/wp-content/uploads/CWBA-Full-Contract.pdf Accessed October 15, 2020. Accessed November 15, 2021, added Sports Initiative and Concerns Regarding Black Women.

Cube, Ice. *Ice Cube Responds to Critics, Addresses Work on Trump's Platinum Plan, Looks to Set Record Straight*. Interview Conducted by Roland Martin. Uploaded by Roland Martin, October 15, 2020. https://youtu.be/vTWTThnXTqA

France, Lisa. "Jay-Z and Meek Mill Launch Prison Reform Organization," cnn.com April 21, 2019. Accessed November 24, 2021. https://www.cnn.com/2019/01/24/entertainment/jay-z-meek-mill-prison/index.html

Garza, Alicia. *The Purpose of Power: How We Come Together When We Fall Apart*. One World/Random House, 2020.

Jay-Z. "The Criminal Justice System Stalks Black People Like Meek Mill," NewYorkTimes.com *New York Times*, November 11, 2017. Accessed November 24, 2021. https://www.nytimes.com/2017/11/17/opinion/jay-z-meek-mill-probation.html

Jeezy feat. Tamika Mallory. "Oh Lord," YJ Music, Inc., Under Exclusive License to Def Jam Recordings, a Division of UMG Recordings, 2020.

Kaba, Mariame. *We Do This Til We Free Us: Abolitionist Organizing and Transforming Justice*. Haymarket Books, 2021.

Lil Baby feat. Tamika Mallory. "The Bigger Picture" Grammy Performance. March 15, 2021. Accessed November 22, 2021. https://youtu.be/zK3PQ_KY_0s

McGrady, Clyde. "Some Famous Rappers Backed Trump's Campaign. Did it Matter?" WashingtonPost.Com. *Washington Post*, November 20, 2020. Accessed November 22, 2021. https://www.washingtonpost.com/lifestyle/rappers-trump-maga-ice-cube-lil-wayne-lil-pump/2020/11/19/f4aec62e-2316-11eb-8599-406466ad-1b8e_story.html

Mallory, Tamika. *Tamika Mallory Was Afraid That Her Grammys Performance Would Be Edited*, Interview Conducted by Tamron Hall. Uploaded by Tamron Hall Show. April 30, 2021. Accessed November 23, 2021. https://youtu.be/yPBCSXb6Xcw

Mill, Meek. "Meek Mill on Criminal Justice Reform, Kanye, New Album." Interview Conducted by Michael Smerconish. https://www.cnn.com/videos/tv/2018/12/01/meek-mill-on-prison-reform-kanye-new-album.cnn Accessed November 28, 2021.

Monae, Janelle and Wondaland Artist Collective. *Hell You Talmbout*. Wondaland Records. August 13, 2015.

Monae, Janelle and African American Policy Forum. *#SayHerName: Hell You Talmbout*, [feat. Prof. Kimberlé Crenshaw, Beyoncé, Alicia Keys, Chloe x Halle, Tierra Whack, Isis V., Zoë Kravitz, Brittany Howard, Asiahn, Mj Rodriguez, Jovian Zayne, Angela Rye, Nikole Hannah-Jones, Brittany Packnett-Cunningham, Alicia Garza] Accessed November 24, 2021. https://www.youtube.com/watch?v=kQbeUN-IfyQ

Nwigwe, Toby. *The Pandemic Project*. August 2020.

Obama, Michelle. "'Unity With Purpose.' Amanda Gorman and Michelle Obama Discuss Art, Identity and Optimism," *Time Magazine*, February 4, 2021. Accessed November 22, 2021. https://time.com/5933596/amanda-gorman-michelle-obama-interview/?fbclid=IwAR1b_KcChYhCU-MwzzqIIg-hCPINi-0J4f_2cP5fdOih_7228SGpcaXm5LOI

Reprise. A Roc Nation Album, Featuring Various artists. 2020.

Saucier, P. Khalil and Tryon Woods. "Hip Hop Studies in Black." *Journal of Popular Music Studies*, Volume 26, Issue 2-3, 2014, pp. 268-294.

Zaru, Deena and LaKeia Brown. "Hip Hop Has Been Standing Up for Black Lives for Decades: 15 Songs and Why They Matter," abcnews.go.com July 12, 2020. Accessed November 27, 2021. https://abcnews.go.com/Entertainment/hip-hop-standing-black-lives-decades-15-songs/story?id=71195591

Author Bios

Elaine Richardson aka Dr. E is Professor of Literacy Studies at The Ohio State University, Columbus, where she teaches in the Department of Teaching and Learning. Her books include *African American Literacies* (Routledge, 2003), focusing on teaching writing from the point of view of African American Language and Literacy traditions, *Hiphop Literacies* (Routledge, 2006), a study of Hiphop language use as an extension of Black folk traditions, and *PHD (Po H# on Dope) to Ph.D.: How Education Saved My Life* (New City Community Press, 2013), an urban educational memoir that chronicles her life from drugs and the street life to the university. Richardson has also co-edited two volumes on African American rhetorical theory, *Understanding African American Rhetoric: Classical Origins to Contemporary Innovations* (Routledge, 2003) and *African American Rhetoric(s): Interdisciplinary Perspectives* (Southern Illinois UP, 2004), and one volume on *Hiphop Feminism—Home Girls Make Some Noise* (Parker Publishing,

2007). Her forthcoming book is titled *Reading the World with Black Girls.* richardson.486@osu.edu

Steve Lessner is Associate Professor of English, Northern Virginia Community College Division of Languages, Arts and Social Sciences. His work focuses on how African American male students' literacy and language practices can be invited, included, and learned from in first-year writing pedagogy, and how Hip Hop artists exhibit specific characteristics of organic intellectuals. slessner@nvcc.edu

'She Ugly': Black Girls, Women in Hiphop and Activism—Hiphop Feminist Literacies Perspectives

Elaine Richardson aka Dr. E

Abstract

This work draws upon Hiphop feminism, studies of Black girlhood, and Black women and girls' literacies to illuminate the layered and violent narratives that shape society's treatment of Black women and girls, what these narratives look like in everyday life, how they are taken up and negotiated in different social spheres, such as an afterschool club for Black middle school girls and the platforms and artistry of women Hiphop artists and creatives. Richardson considers what activism is possible through juxtaposing Black girls as emerging creatives, celebrity corporate artist activists Nicki Minaj and Cardi B, independent activist artists such as Noname and dream hampton. Given the far-reaching representations of Black women and girls in popular culture, the art, lives and platforms of women in Hiphop are critical sites to understanding complexities, strategies and possibilities for social change.

Keywords

Hiphop Feminism, Black girls' and women's literacies, Hiphop women artists, performance activism, social justice, Nicki Minaj, Cardi B, Noname, dream hampton

"She ugly. If you don't know when somebody ugly, I don't know what to tell you. She had surgery. Some people are ugly. She ugly and she nasty."

That was Nicole's case closed slam dunk statement on the matter. We had just watched a music video "Letter to Nicki Minaj" that came out during the 2012-2013 school year. It featured a group of young Black girl performers called Watoto from the Nile. Their 2012 Kickstarter campaign page describes them as "A group of young princesses from their hometown of Harriet Tubman City (Baltimore, Maryland). They have come to breathe life back into a destructive music culture that's on life support."[1]

Around the time of "Letter to Nicki Minaj," the core of the group was comprised of 3 sisters Nia (12), Nya (11), and Kamaria (7), and another girl, Mary Angel (12). The oeuvre of their work speaks to social injustices against Black people. The group is mentored by the sisters' father with a strong Afrocentric emphasis. Watoto has songs

---

1. https://www.kickstarter.com/projects/watoto/help-watoto-from-the-nile-kickstart-the-love-proje/description.

about police brutality, violence, misogynoir (Black racialized and gendered misogyny, Bailey) in Hiphop, Black Lives Matter-a dedication to Trayvon Martin, the benefits of a plant-based diet, and more. I purposefully shared this video with my afterschool club girls because it featured Black girls close to their own ages, who were creating a public platform using performance arts to share their opinions about things that concerned their lives and their communities. The video fit with the Black and Hiphop feminist performance-based approach I was implementing.

During the time of the club (2010-2015) – and unfortunately, throughout history, and currently – Black women and girls BE facing down discourses NOT of our own making that empower everybody but us! I'm deeply invested in doing my part, to push against structural barriers and narratives, to make visible complex mundane "truths" that are killing us, like "She ugly." As such, I come at this work, as a Black woman literacy scholar in community with my community; and I don't know who all needs to hear this, but: WE TIRED.

Black Women and Girls' Literacies: on Our Own Terms

We tired of the traditional narrow view that promotes literacy as a print bound, politically neutral, private mental activity, where letters correspond to sounds, and sounds to words, and reading and meaning making are universal and context-free. Who beautiful? How YOU define beauty? Who smart? Who is a good girl or woman? Who is worthy? How you answer these questions is informed by your identity, the images, patterns, and words you've internalized from the social activities in which you have participated, from school, from media, your life experiences, your history. The sense you make and the meanings you identify with are informed by your socialization. The ideas, myths, attitudes and values you hold are programmed into you. Critical literacy is the search for truth through interrogating what we've been fed. We must ask ourselves who told us that and why? Who is empowered or disempowered by certain knowledge and social arrangements? For example, Black women's and girls' so-called inherent "at-riskness," in particular, is socially constructed. This means there's a whole web of social practices related to economic, political, patriarchal, cultural, racist and sexist arrangements that continually hold us down.

The mission of Black community literacies education is to interrupt racism, sexism, classism, cultural conflict, and social inequality. In my Black critical Hiphop feminist literacies approach, I use storytelling, viral and rap music videos, artmaking, news media, documentaries, short literature pieces, performance, creative writing, and dialogic inquiry to center our lived experiences and activate our creativity for the purposes of our collective empowerment. Drawing upon Hiphop feminism, studies of Black girlhood and Black women and girls' literacies, I focus on how Black women and girls advance and protect ourselves and our loved ones in society, strategies we use to make meaning and assert ourselves in the face of violent systems of power (Richardson). Hiphop feminist literacies work thwarts violence against Black women and girls and centers herstories (Lindsey). The focus is upon the creative potential of Black girlhood (Brown). It's also about our joy, pleasure, and love. In 2000,

Joan Morgan, the thinker that described and defined Hiphop feminism, highlighted the grayness of the perspectives that manifested in her own life and in young Black women of that era.[2] Kierna Mayo says of the late 1980's and the 1990's Hiphop feminist generation:

> We manifested the politics of a spanking-new Black feminism and told her she could bring alla her homies—contradiction, agency, image, desire, power, media, sex, white folks—to the hood and the academy. And we did all this while steeped in a cultural ecosystem that was developing at warp speed, fueled by the machinations of young men that were often toxic. Young men that we loved. (x)

Then and now, Black women and girls are entangled in patriarchal systems with our brothers, sons, and loved ones. We are expected to be sources of love, loyalty, and labor, even when being the source may be harmful. This expectation is manifested by the general society in which Black people and Hiphop are entangled. This is the grayness of life. Hiphop feminist-informed community literacy work holds space for women and girls of color to work through our experiences and imagine better for ourselves individually and collectively. As a Black Hiphop feminist literacies performance activist, I facilitate Black girlhood as a space of creativity (Brown). I ask: What power can be harnessed if we see our girls and ourselves as creatives? What activism is possible from commercial corporate celebrity artists? What can we learn from looking at artists as activists? Not every artist is an organizer, but artists have fans, followers, platforms, and are social influencers. The messages they convey in their art and lives are far-reaching and important sites of critical inquiry.

The Making of Black Girl Activist Artists

Our work in the club was about us creating our own brand of powerful self-literacy education and teasing out the threads of critical social justice possibilities in Black popular culture and in ourselves, even as both are tied to violence. So, Nicole's slam dunk seemingly self-evident "fact" about Nicki Minaj, "she ugly," is a statement not to be written off or taken lightly.

"But where do we get that from? Where did that come from? Why do we call each other ugly?" I ask.

Georgia chimes in low-rating Nicki Minaj as a person and an artist, "She ratchet and she can't rap."

"Can you beat her"? I ask.

---

2. For a thorough review of Hiphop feminism from Tricia Rose and Joan Morgan to the contemporary cadre of Hiphop feminist scholarship and activism See Halliday, Aria and Ashley N. Payne's Introduction: Savage and Savvy: Mapping Contemporary Hip Hop Feminism. "Twenty-First Century B.I.T.C.H. Frameworks: Hip Hop Feminism Comes of Age," *Journal of Hip Hop Studies*, Vol. 7, Iss. 1, 2020. pp. 8-18.

"I can beat her. I can rap betta than that if you give me some words to rap on," Georgia says with conviction.

My tones rise to match hers, "I'm giving you words, by showing this video."

"Nicki Minaj CAN rap and I love her. I watch her videos over and over," says Maelynn.

"That's for dudes," says Georgia, just as matter-of-factly as she pleases. "Why Nicki Minaj wanna be like ratchedness and dirty and having on no clothes? I'm not gay bruh!"

I say, "If Nicki Minaj was in here right now, you wouldn't be saying none of that."

Mya speaks her thoughts in a quiet timid voice. "I watch it over and over too and I'm not gay."

"Thanks for keepin it real," Maelynn replied as though she was a defense attorney, pleased by the contribution of her star witness.

I turn and scan the whole group of about 14 girls on that day, to encourage them all to speak. "Why did Watoto from the Nile make the video? What is "Letter to Nicki Minaj" about?"

Maelynn jumps right in. "The girls singing about how Nicki a star, and how all the young girls in school wanna be just like her. She should use her power for the community. Girls shouldn't look up to her as a good person."

Again, scanning the room in hopes of including more voices, I ask, "How do we know if she a good person from her performance?

Then an argument starts.

Georgia: "She ratchet!"

Nicole: "I on't like her."

Maelynn: "Who cares. Shut up"!

Geogia, Nicole and Maelynn were friends and three of the strongest personalities. One of my roles as facilitator of the club is to hold space for all of the girls and give them a chance to voice their thoughts but also to redirect and keep them focused. I threw up my hand to try to head off a negative argument and keep us connected to the purpose of the group. I posed a question:

"Do y'all remember when we watched *The Black Girl Project*? Remember our talk about Black women and girls and our ongoing fight for social change? Anybody got any notes on that? What are some of the ideas in the Watoto song that show some of the same issues we been going through in our history?"

"About class mobility"? Tamia offered up for our consideration.

"Umm," I say. "Ok, speak on it! How does "Letter to Nicki" relate to class mobility?"

"Moving up in life," said Kat.

"Ok, good. She said moving up in life. Isn't Nicki Minaj being successful and moving up in her life? How do we as Black women and girls and our community move up in life? A person moving up as an individual doesn't necessarily help other people in our community move up. How do we move up together?"

"By having a good job," Lizzie says.

"Ok. But you having a good job gonna help us all move up?" I asked, as I stood up to move around the room.

"Having a education," Georgia says, and I smile at her because I am pleased that they dropped the argument, and she is in the dialogue!

Walking over near Georgia, I respond, "Education is gooood, but we need the right education, that helps us as a people."

"Havin a dream," Lizzie says.

Lizzie's answer recalls the contribution of our brilliant and beloved Civil Rights Leader, Dr. Martin Luther King. This answer in a conversation on social change is great; but I am pushing the girls to recount key ideas from the *Black Girl Project*. The documentary explicitly spoke of Black women and girls as pathbreakers in science, education, culture, entertainment, and government, accompanied by images of Oprah, Michelle Obama, Shirley Chisolm, Beyonce, Lil Kim, and Alicia Keys. Yet the documentary raised an important question that we spent ample time on: "But does any of that matter when we are still looked upon as mules, mammies, and the workhorses of the world?" So, I respond to Lizzie and the entire group:

"I mean it's good to have a job, a dream and education, but what are some concrete ways, that we can make differences in our community and our own lives, change stuff that's not right, like how Black women fought for us as Black people to get free, to vote, to have rights, and support the needs of Black women and girls as a group."

Georgia asks, "Can we watch that video again?"

She does not like my reply, "We can. But not at this moment."

"Err! [she goes imitating screeching tires]. You bootleg!" She decries.

"Sorry if you didn't catch it or were absent that day. I'll show it again, but right now I know somebody in here remembers the one girl who was talking about how reading W.E.B. DuBois helped her learn that Black people can have power through social change. What does that mean? To have power through social change?"

"She said direct change," Kat says. "She said a lot of his readings talk about you can only have direct change from political power."

That got Nicole's attention. "Who said that?"

Summoning Kat with my right hand in Baptist tambourine flair, "Say it again, Kat."

Kat obliged in a cool voice of knowing, "The girl in *Black Girl Project* said she learned that from reading W. E. B. Dubois, a Black sociologist."

"I remember some of y'all talked about things you wanted to see changed. Y'all said y'all want people to stop calling Black girls names, like baldheaded, for school to stop suspending people, and teachers to listen more. These are important issues about how y'all are treated. We said we were gonna organize, do creative projects and present them to the school."

Black Girls and Women: Desired, Despised and (In)Disposable

The range of responses to Nicki Minaj[3] praised and castigated her as a star and personally, largely revealing Nicole's and Georgia's moves for affirmation and the contradiction of the Black rhetorical condition. This is a condition where Black bodies are despised for not being so-called normal and desired as essential to the political economy. Nicole, one of the girls castigating Nicki, had access to light-skinned privilege. But she also experienced discrimination because she identified as lesbian. Georgia was lightskinned as well, but known as a bully and a "struggling reader." Nicole had to defend herself a lot, fending off boys who picked on her. She was suspended often, which broke my heart, as she was a star when she was able to participate in the club. Similarly, I saw the star power in Georgia. Both of these girls challenged me in different ways to be the best and learn from them how to bring the best out of them and myself.

In the larger school system, both of these girls were marked as "bad" and at-risk for the school-to-prison pipeline and other forms of containment. Their lives reflect the Black rhetorical condition as well as align with the *Black Girl Project*'s view that Black girls and women are exploited as mules, mammies, and workhorses of the world, having to work twice as hard to be valued yet devalued. The sentiment, if not, the words, the girls assigned to Nicki Minaj ugly, nasty, ratchet, dirty, naked, having surgery, bears this out as well. Additionally, Georgia's insinuation that girls who find pleasure in Nicki's performances are gay, marks same gender adoration as aberrant. This is not to say that Nicki's "ratchet" performance in 'Stupid Hoe" (the song and video that Watoto of the Nile target) should not be critiqued. It is messy and gray, not as black and white as any of us may like it to be. And for those consumers who love her performance gay or not, more power to them.

The song disses Lil Kim, aka the Queen B. Kim gained wide-recognition in the mid 1990s with Biggie Smalls and the Junior Mafia camp. Kim and Nicki had ongoing beef ever since Nicki dropped a mix tape around 2007, with an image of herself on the cover, that was a definite "bite" off Lil Kim's "Hardcore" album cover. During the time when Nicki dropped "Stupid Hoe" (2012ish) ratchet was almost synonymous with 'classless.' Of course, like most Black slang, "ratchet" has changed rapidly and has a range of meaning potentials depending on who is saying what, when, where and to whom. Middle class Black folks can perform and find joy in ratchet performance and critique notions of anti-Blackness and (anti) respectability (Lane). Respectability is always held over the heads of working class Black people perceived as not measuring up to middle-class Blackness.

I identify with working class Black people, even though I have earned a Ph.D. in English and Applied Linguistics. We are seen as the personification of lowness, rather than performing narratives that underlie oppressive systems, neither of our own making. I am thinking particularly about my one-woman show and book from *Po Ho on Dope to Ph.D.* I understand performance as survival. Ratchetness is a form of social currency. Human beings that perform ratchetness are not illegal nor illiterate. Some-

---

3. https://en.wikipedia.org/wiki/Nicki_Minaj.

times a girl has to do what she must. We are incorporated into a punitive culture of varying realms of anti-Black woman violence, from the performances of Nicki Minaj, to young Black girls, all trying to find their way to power.

So, when Georgia and Nicole started dissin Nicki, I tried to redirect their thinking to our collective humanity and to how they themselves experience violence every day: when they are called names, such as baldheaded, by those who want to diss and degrade their humanity; when teachers don't understand or have time to listen to their experiences; when suspension is the schools' answer to Black girls' unmet needs. These Black girls and masses across the country live in communities that continue to suffer intergenerationally from decades of federal, state and local policies that disadvantage them. I'm not alone in recognizing this. Black feminist scholar Aria Halliday reminds us of "how the histories of subjugation, degradation, and subsequent stereotyping of Black women affect how [Black women and girls'] bodies are made visible, invisible, and hypervisible in the media..." (78). Sensibilities normalize the economies of rape culture and Black girls' socialization into existing power structures.

For me, rape culture is about people in power taking advantage and exploiting "weaker" people. Rape is entangled with capitalist exploitation. This includes countries that underdevelop "third world" peoples and take their natural resources, environments where rape is rampant and normal and people who get raped are blamed. Rape is powerful when a powerful and well-resourced country systemically withholds social goods from people because they are not able to pay, or they are not seen as worthy because they have been racialized, or made outcasts because of their gender and sexuality.

I understand racialized gender and sexuality are part of power structures in my usage and refers to the diminishment of people of color because they have been othered, negatively sexualized and gendered, as they are not white middle-class and heterosexual. This racialization and stigmatization of people because they are not white, middle-class, or seen as less than human because of their gender and sexuality is made to seem normal. It is an acceptable form of hatred used to deprive people of rights, privileges, goods and services. Personal achievement narratives also create power structures that uphold the violent system of capitalism which is based on the myth that some people are better and worth more than others, because of their individual hard work. The hard work that many people do to stay alive is discounted though it is essential life blood for the system of sexist racial capitalist inequality. It is difficult to focus on the violence of capitalism because it is intertwined with social progress, mobility and leisure. For collective power building work that brings us together, Alicia Garza, one of the founders of Black Lives Matter, urges that we must learn and unlearn about each other to create strong alliances based on "differently experienced yet connected exploitation and oppression" (150).

In this particular conversation with the girls, I tried to prevent erasure of Nicki Minaj the performer and person and encourage them to think beyond the binaries, to which we've become accustomed. Because of the constraints within which I worked, in the afterschool space with middle school girls, I was not able to engage more deeply the ways that Nicki's performance could be considered an attempt to clap back at racialized sexual and gender ideas of beauty and sexuality. What I did was try to center us in art as a mode of inquiry, resistance, creativity and freedom. My commentary as well as ongoing work with women and girls and my own self seeks to illuminate and refuse violence against us; center the need for us to strive to love our whole selves and each other and develop critical consciousness; and focus toward working for concrete change in our community.

The girls of Watoto from the Nile rap and sing a song that encourages Nicki Minaj to use the power of her celebrity as a Hiphop artist with a huge platform to lead young girls to fight for their liberation. The representations of Nicki's performance in Watoto's song and video highlight her star status, alluring sexuality, revealing clothing, spectacular performance of sexual and music industry bondage/freedom. Watoto also highlights Nicki as a Harriet Tubman figure, a linkage to Black women and girls' historic struggle against systems of exploitation. They illuminated Nicki as a purveyor of stereotypes of Black sexuality and framed her within the dehumanizing white male enslaver gaze of Black feminine sexuality. This is a widespread practice rooted in slavery which polices, criminalizes, and exploits Black women and girls' bodies and lives.

What can we learn from taking a closer look at Black women Hiphop artists as celebrity corporate artists as activist and independent artist activists?

Celebrity Corporate Artist as Activist: Nicki Minaj

Like many other Black celebrity Hiphop artists, Trinidadian born and Queens, New York-bred, Nicki Minaj started life in humble beginnings. She came up the ranks through mixtapes and made her way to be the first woman rapper signed to Young Money Records. She is a highly skilled and carefully crafted commercial Hiphop music industry artist. She is beautiful and voluptuous. Her lyrics are filled with braggadoccio. She is known for creative, if sometimes controversial, persona. She has amassed pop cross-over appeal and a high standard of living for herself and her family. Among Nicki's stances, she has spoken out about white cultural appropriation of Black culture, in particular how Black artists are snubbed and devalued, while white artists are rewarded (VanDerWerff). Because of her solidarity on issues of women's and LGBTQ rights, in 2019, she pulled out of tour in Saudi Arabia (Associated Press).

She has also donated proceeds from one of her songs to the Bail Project, which works to end cash bail and disrupt mass incarceration (Wikipedia). Her philanthropic efforts include financing clean water wells to villages in Chennai, India[4], as well as providing college scholarships and loan repayments for students through her initiative, "Student of The Game" (Bailey).

Nicki is a complex artist and Black woman in America. She is good, sometimes makes bad decisions, but not ugly. It is clear that she has a penchant for supporting her men relatives and friends regardless of their violence against women and girls. She fell under scrutiny when she bailed out her brother, in 2015, on charges of sexually assaulting his then 11-year-old stepdaughter. Her brother was recently convicted

---

4. https://www.looktothestars.org/news/18084-nicki-minaj-awards-37-college-scholarships.

and sentenced to 25 years in prison (Onley). Similarly, Nicki has stood by her husband who in 1995 pled guilty to attempted rape (to avoid the charge of first-degree rape that occurred in 1994). The woman who accused Nicki Minaj's husband of rape has alleged that Minaj offered her money to recant her story as well as harassed her. The woman is now suing Nicki Minaj. Her husband has also been recently charged for not registering himself as a sex offender in the state of California for which he will face sentencing. Further down this trail and tale is that:

> Minaj previously defended [her husband], writing in reference to the alleged rape, which occurred when Hough [the victim] was 16: "He was 15, she was 16 … in a relationship . . . But go awf, internet, y'all can't run my life. y'all can't even run y'all own life." [Minaj] has previously worked with and defended [fellow rapper] 6ix9ine, who pleaded guilty to the use of a child in a sexual performance in 2015. (Juzwiak)

Furthermore, Nicki has been rebuked for reckless use of her twitter platform of over 22 million followers. She tweeted that her cousin's friend in Trinidad became impotent after being vaccinated and that she wasn't going to the Met Gala because she didn't do enough research to feel comfortable to take the vaccine. She was confronted by Anthony Fauci, Chief Medical Advisor to President Biden, and Joy Reid, a well-respected Black woman MSNBC Correspondent, among others. Joy Reid stated that although Black people should be skeptical of a mandated vaccine, given the treatment of Blacks in this country, conspiracy theories have been debunked by science. Reid expressed sadness that Nicki used her platform in a way that might encourage already vulnerable Black people to not get the vaccine (Adams).

Looking at Nicki Minaj as a celebrity corporate artist as activist highlights how her complex positionality plays out in her performance around critical social justice actions. It is equally important to take into consideration how we are all socially positioned, by our beliefs, psychological status and spiritual clarity. Reading the world with Black girls through a popular woman Hiphop artist, such as Nicki Minaj, presents the opportunity to examine our self-interests, self-investments, self-determination, and the ways that the white power structure and corporate patriarchal interests penetrate how we see each other and ourselves. Reading Nicki's performance art and her life should help us think more creatively about how to get free. We must read against the patriarchy and create what we need.

Independent Artist Activist: Noname

As an independent rapper, not tied to a major corporate label, Noname[5] may be more explicitly legible as an activist artist, rather than a celebrity artist as activist. Her fellow Chicagoan and phenomenal independent artist Chance the Rapper featured her on the track "Lost" on his 2013 mixtape *Acid Rap*. It was downloaded over one mil-

---

5. https://en.wikipedia.org/wiki/Noname_(rapper).

lion times.[6] In 2016, she shined again on Chance's Grammy-winning *Coloring Book*. She dropped her own critically acclaimed debut, *Telefone*, in 2017. These moves provided wider recognition for Noname, and the means to become a self-sustained artist, with creative control over her brand and the music and politics she chooses to share. "I wish there was a different narrative of what rappers can be. We're only pitched to aspire to be almost unnecessarily wealthy," she tells music reporter, Dan Rys.[7] I think "unnecessarily wealthy" is a valuable idea. For me, it conjures the idea of necessary wealth, capitalism as a tool, rather than a means to an end. Another narrative Noname pushes against is myths of women in Hiphop and conscious rap, that pit them against each other, to the detriment of their collective power. She has written about horniness, her first time, a failed love affair, and used her vagina as a powerful character in her lyrics on her *Room 25* project. She says she used the word "pussy" around a thousand times in it. "A lot of my fans . . . I think they like me because they think I'm the anti-Cardi B. I'm not," Noname tells Rawiya Kameir in *The Fader*.[8] I think Noname deliberately wrote songs celebrating her sexuality to show solidarity with Black women rappers whose bread and butter is portraying their sexuality in their music. And to let them know she sees them as whole persons and much more than their performances.

Though she is not the anti-Cardi B, and I would add, nor the anti-Nicki Minaj, fame is not the end game for her, at least not to the point where she is "taking up unnecessary space".[9] She seeks to attract people to political education through her brand of music and art. As someone who was a slow reader in school, being fed "fictitious bullshit," she found slam poetry and the rest is history.[10] She became attracted to revolutionary concepts and ideas through enjoyable art, music and film that can be seen and heard. Her creation of Noname Book Club comes out of her experience. The book club is a space to discuss social justice literature and donate books to prisons. She raises money through Patreon to send monthly book picks to prisons and to pay facilitators, staff, graphic artists, who work to curate high quality monthly book discussions. Book club meetups are online because of COVID-19. There are book club chapters in major cities throughout the United States and one in London. Noname Book Club has partnerships with libraries around the country to make sure monthly book club picks are available for free (nonamebooks.com).

Her artistry and community building outreach are intertwined with her quest to understand and thwart inequitable systems. She uses Twitter to connect with liberation movements and revolutionary thinkers such as longtime prison industrial com-

---

6. https://www.insider.com/who-is-chance-the-rapper-2017-4#a-few-months-later-childish-gambino-donald-glover-featured-him-on-his-song-they-dont-like-me-3.

7. https://www.billboard.com/articles/columns/hip-hop/8508730/noname-indie-now-artist-interview.

8. https://www.thefader.com/2018/09/11/noname-room-25-interview.

9. https://www.npr.org/2020/12/19/948005131/i-want-us-to-dream-a-little-bigger-noname-and-mariame-kaba-on-art-and-abolition.

10. https://www.thefader.com/2018/09/11/noname-room-25-interview.

plex [PIC] abolition organizer Mariame Kaba @prisonculture.[11] "PIC abolition is a positive project that focuses, in part, on building a society where it is possible to address harm without relying on structural forms of oppression or the violent systems that increase it" (Kaba 2).

In a beautiful conversation between Noname and Mariame Kaba about the role of art in abolition, Kaba explains that we need art such as Hiphop to help transform our world.[12] She believes we all have that responsibility, to make the world better. At the same time, Kaba acknowledges "not everybody's an organizer, and that's OK." But when artists do create art that helps people think differently, "it can help disrupt patterns and old ways of thinking." Of her fellow Hiphop artists, Noname ruminates, "I just want us to dream a little bit bigger than reform." I feel a bit of frustration in her reply, since she bemoans the power of Hiphop artists to bring people together, but largely for their own capitalist gains. "That's all I'm wanting from us — from hip-hop artists as a community. I think a lot of it is because folks don't have people around them challenging them," Noname reflects.

The wise Kaba agrees that a major problem with celebrities is that they must be self-regulated, self-accountable, and tied to organizations. With regard to Kaba's abolitionist praxis, Naomi Murakawa attests:

> Kaba's abolitionist vision burns so bright precisely because she refuses to be the single star, dazzling alone. Why be a star when you can make a constellation? …[A] constellation of co-organizers, cofounders, and coconspirators, together in abolitionist practice of refusal, care, and collectivity. (xviii)

In alignment with this philosophy and movement, Noname honors Hiphop's origins in collective struggle. She believes this art form was created for Black liberation, to share the message of what is going on in our communities. "Because a community that I come from made this work, and now I'm able to sustain myself, I feel it's my responsibility to be as honest and radical in my music as I possibly can".[13]

Celebrity Artist as Activist: Cardi B

Cardi B is no less honest and radical, if not in her music, then certainly in her representations, her critical commentary on the politics of feminism, the music industry, conservatism, racism and more. She is a Black Latina rap star, who made a name for herself in reality TV on *Love & Hip Hop: New York*.[14] Cardi B doesn't embrace traditional ideologies of feminism or respectability. She represents a naked truth that resonates with the life experiences of today's Hiphop and Black Lives Matter generations,

---

11. https://www.npr.org/2020/12/19/948005131/i-want-us-to-dream-a-little-bigger-noname-and-mariame-kaba-on-art-and-abolition.

12. https://www.npr.org/2020/12/19/948005131/i-want-us-to-dream-a-little-bigger-noname-and-mariame-kaba-on-art-and-abolition.

13. https://www.npr.org/2020/12/19/948005131/i-want-us-to-dream-a-little-bigger-noname-and-mariame-kaba-on-art-and-abolition.

14. https://en.wikipedia.org/wiki/Cardi_B

in her unashamed journey from stripping to chart topping celebrity artist. She gets "the bag"[15] and works to support her community. In 2018, *Time Magazine* named her one of the 100 most influential people in the world.

In her 2017 piece, "Cardi B Love & Hiphop's Unlikely Feminist Hero," Sherri Williams writes about the powerful activist work that Cardi B does through pop culture and social media. Williams suggests that Cardi B should be enlisted in the feminist movement. In particular, Williams cites Cardi B's November 2016 Instagram post that reached millions of her followers that might not otherwise fathom (Black) feminism:

> If you believe in equal rights for women, that makes you a feminist. I don't understand how you bitches feel like being a feminist is a woman that have a education, that have a degree. That is not being a feminist. You discouraging a certain type of woman, that certainly doesn't make you one. Some bitches wanna act like "oh you have to read a book about feminists." That's only a definition for a simple word. The problem is that being a feminist is something so great and y'all don't want me to be great but too bad. Because at the end of the day I'm going to encourage any type of woman. You don't have to be a woman like me to encourage and support you and tell you "yes bitch, keep on going." And that's why you mad you little dusty ass bitch.

Cardi B claps back on a narrowly defined view of her literacy, as relegated to reading "a book about feminists." This strand of her literacy work is in the lineage of the great abolitionist Sojourner Truth. The liberatory mindset of abolitionist and women's rights activist, Sojourner Truth, could not be contained by conventional definitions of literacy that can be measured on standardized tests. The standard conception of literacy stratifies human beings and reproduces harm. Sojourner Truth's readings of "men and nations" resists and confronts stratifying white patriarchal systems. In "Woman Suffrage," Truth is reported to have said:

> … I don't read such small stuff as letters, I read men and nations. I can see through a millstone, though I can't see through a spelling-book. What a narrow idea a reading qualification is for a voter! I know and do what is right better than many big men who read. (Painter 230)

Truth's actions on behalf of self-preservation and collective uplift of Black lives, her critical feminist literacies, challenged patriarchy, enslavement, sexism, racism, and disenfranchisement. Unlike Truth, Cardi B is literate in the narrow sense required of high school graduates in the current system, what Noname coined "fictitious bullshit" reading. Like Sojourner Truth, Cardi B reads men and nations for the collective good of women and humanity.

Like Nicki Minaj and many other Black women artists, Cardi B has been denigrated for having cosmetic surgery. One strand of thought among Black folks is the stigma of selling out or not being natural. Depending on the type of cosmetic surgery, selling out would be changing one's body to gain access to higher value in the market, based on certain dominant conceptions of beauty and worth. With regard to having

---

15. Hiphop slang term for wealth or money.

butt surgery, the last time I checked, large and shapely butts are highly desirable as a Black beauty mark.

Rather than continue down this trail of beauty marks and recreated body parts, the point is all of us have the right to bodily autonomy. And as Black feminist activist Tanya Fields shared "Radical Black Joy is inherent as a human need and not some special trinket you get after you rise high enough on the socioeconomic ladder or unlock some special level of desirability or accomplishment" (29). Generating spaces of Black joy and affirmation helps us to see ourselves with clarity. Our worth is inherent. We are not defined by market values and white Anglo aesthetics. Whether we decide to get surgery or not, we have to be spiritually healthy and self-loving. At the end of the day, we are all performing and complicit with the market on some level.

In Cardi B's Foreword to activist Tamika D. Mallory's book,[16] *Is There Room for Someone Like Me?*, Cardi ponders if she is a fit for movement work. She describes herself as "a real-ass bitch" who feels compelled to speak out about injustice. "Yes, I'm a rapper. Yes, I twerk. No, I'm not trying to be your children's role model" (xxii). Presenting herself this way addresses the mindset of the shut up and rap, strip, run or dribble sentiment of conservative critics. They want Black artists and athletes to get the bag and run! Colin Kaepernick and LeBron James are arguably the most iconic athletes of this generation who reject this sentiment. Along with artists such as Cardi B, they stand up, speak out, kneel, twerk, and otherwise advocate for racial justice. They want a country where the masses have their basic needs met, e.g. healthy food, clean water, housing, education, healthcare, art, joy, and a non-violence-based society. Cardi B is "a real-ass bitch" and a damn good one, as we used to say.

Though they have different experiences and neither woman is perfect, Cardi B is as important, if not moreso, as an activist as is Michelle Obama. Both know the metaphysical dilemma of bein alive, bein a woman and bein colored (Shange). They both experience misogynoir (Bailey) and have some stake in the freedom of Black people. Their politics inform their identities and influence how people react to them. Both have inspirational stories that are about belonging. Both are celebrities with massive social reach and cachet with their respective constituencies. Both are political actors, whether they, or others, deem them so or not.

Michelle Obama wants to be read as non-political in her story of personal achievement and perseverance against Chicago's racism. She tells the story of opportunities that were not afforded suffering adults and foreparents in her life, such as attending a magnet high school, that set her on the path to Princeton, Harvard Law School, a six-figure salary, and beyond. She also spills secrets, such as smoking marijuana and pre-marital sex as a youth, that make her relatable to everyday people. She made it because of her family's commitment to her and her brother's success and their teachings of positive thinking. Keeanga Yamahtta Taylor shows up the problem with this narrative:

---

16. Mallory, Tamika, D. State of Emergency: How We Win in the Country We Built (as told to Ashley A. Coleman), Black Privilege Publishing, Atria, 2021.

> ... Obama's own emphasis on striving as a way to overcome racial discrimination ... reduces racial inequality to one of psychological impairment that can be overcome through sheer determination and a positive attitude. She fails to see how it was bitter struggle against real institutions that created the new world she was able to thrive in.

Michelle Obama's message resonates with all kinds of women, especially Black women. As Taylor reminds us:

> Indeed, black women in this country are so debased and ignored that it often feels as if the success and public adoration of Obama can lift and make visible all black women—a process Obama herself encourages.

Cardi B may not have as wide an appeal as Michelle Obama, but her story is potent and connects with masses. She tells of growing up in a very strict home in her Bronx community. She describes herself as a loud kid who was full of confidence. Her inspiration to succeed was not wanting to go through what her mother went through. She always wanted to be an artist. She graduated high school and rebelled against her mother's rules and her mom kicked her out. Cardi went to college but did not finish ("See Her, Hear Her: Celebrating Women in Music"). She worked as a cashier and then as a stripper to become financially independent and escape an abusive boyfriend. She used that money to invest in her music career (Decker et al.). She describes herself as someone from the bottom, where it's a struggle to not be killed (B, Cardi).

Cardi B's struggle and rise to fame is what drives her to use her voice for those still in the bottom. A social media post by a former high school teacher speaks of Cardi B's political impact and intellect:

> For those of you on my feed who are trashing Cardi B for representing a political voice a) she probably scored higher than you on the US History regents' exam and was in my AP govt class b) you're not nearly as busy as her, and what have you done to advance political discourse in this country? C) She has a national platform and is using it to speak about things that are important... why can't we respect that? d) STFU and take a seat. (Tinubu)

Cardi B's platform brings awareness to millions "with a single tweet, with a single social media post, with a single sound bite…" (xiii). Even so, she is less legible to many as a political force than Michelle Obama. Even with all of her clout, rap moguls such as Jermaine Dupri assessed women rappers such as Cardi B as not having any skills and just being a stripper rapper. To that, Cardi speaks to the conditioning of audiences:

> ... First of all, I rap about my pussy because she my best friend, you know what I'm saying. And second of all it's because it seems like that's what people wanna hear. I ain't even gonna front because let me tell you something, when I did "Be Careful," people was talking madd shit in the beginning. ... 'What the fuck is this? This is not what I expected. I expected this. I expected that. ... So I'm like, if that's what people ain't tryna hear, then alright. Then

I'mma start rapping about my pussy again. ... There's a lot of female rappers that be rappin they ass off and don't be talking about they pussy, and don't be talking about getting down and dirty. Y'all don't be supporting them. ... And they be madd dope. These bloggers don't support them. They don't give them the recognition. So, don't blame that shit on us, when y'all not the ones that's supporting them.[17]

I don't see rappers such as Cardi B and Megan Thee Stallion acquiescing to stereotypes, as much as I see them capitalizing off their moment. They gettin in where they fit in. They are not fighting to change the music industry. But they speak out and advocate on social issues. Cardi B campaigned for Bernie Sanders. In 2020, she interviewed him on her Instagram and Twitter to represent and educate her followers. She also spoke out against conservative Black woman republican activist Candice Owens who railed against her, calling her "illiterate" and irresponsible for using her platform to support Joe Biden, who played a role in mass incarceration.[18] Owens also bashed Cardi B and Megan Thee Stallion for their celebration of women's sexual pleasure song "WAP". Owens argues that the song is destroying the values of the Black community.

Megan Thee Stallion is set to graduate college with an undergraduate degree in Health Administration as of this writing and plans to go into building assisted living facilities. After allegedly being shot in both her feet by a Black male rapper, Torey Lanez, Megan discussed how she was expected to keep silent, be strong and not disclose her trauma or the identity of Lanez. She was already a supporter of Black women but this incident caused her to speak out more forcefully as an advocate for the protection of Black women. Megan published a powerful opinion piece in the *New York Times*, "Why I Speak Up for Black Woman." The piece addresses stereotypes, the many disparities Black women face, the lack of widespread education on the many contributions Black women have made in sociey. She also spoke out against Daniel Cameron, the Black Republican Attorney General, who did not indict the Louisville Kentucky police, that killed the young Black woman emergency medical technician Breonna Taylor in a botched raid.

But this passage from Megan's piece confronts why going after Black women rappers for portraying their sexuality misses the mark:

I've received quite a bit of attention for appearance as well as my talent. I choose my own clothing. Let me repeat: I choose what I wear, not because I am trying to appeal to men, but because I am showing pride in my appearance, and a positive body image is central to who I am as a woman and a performer. I value compliments from women far more than from men. But the remarks about how I choose to present myself have often been judgmental and cruel, with many assuming that I'm dressing and performing for the

---

17. Cardi B responds to Jermaine Dupri's comments on female rappers, July 12, 2019. https://twitter.com/i/events/1149584118851575808?ref_src=twsrc%5Etfw.

18. https://www.billboard.com/articles/columns/hip-hop/9446762/cardi-b-candace-owens-political-debate-timeline/.

male gaze. When women choose to capitalize on our sexuality, to reclaim our *own* power, like I have, we are vilified and disrespected.

To protect children from materials that they are too young to critically process in this wide open digital information society is nearly impossible. This is not to excuse the corporate music industry as well as Hollywood that slot women and girls of color into certain sales categories and formulas that they created for maximum profit. Following bell hooks, I call it selling hot pussy. Hot P structures feed the mindset that other aspects of women's and girls' humanity are not worth as much (hooks).

Artists such as Megan and Cardi B are seen as street hookers in the parlance of conservative forces who want to put fear into (white) Christian fundamentalists or win over Black Democrats. It is not surprising that Cardi B asks legendary activist Angela Davis, co-foreword writer to Tamika Mallory's book, where do people like her fit in movement work? Davis extols:

> It is important that you and people like you, our artists, cultural workers, and influencers of new generations, are present because you invite critical engagement with our current issues. … Hip-hop like everything else, is diverse and full of internal contradictions, but it is absolutely clear that this music has helped to create new communities of struggle. … Most often it is the forgers of our popular musical and visual cultures who know how to invite the world to experience, at the level of feeling, desires for habitable futures that scholars have not figured out how to convey. (xvi-xvii)

Independent Activist Artist: dream hampton

Her love for the Detroit hood of her nurture. Her near rape at age 12.[19] The verbal violence that gripped her in the mid 1980s rap battle between Roxanne Shante and the Real Roxanne. Her coming of age during the devastation of the Black community by crack cocaine to the sounds of rap. Graduated from NYU's Tisch School of the Arts. Her profiles of up-and-coming Hiphop artists and stars in rap rags provided insight. Her writings about police brutality, misogynoir in rap, and the politics of the music industry, raised awareness among the young and elders. Highly productive soul she is. Her passion is for producing justice-oriented films and documentaries. One of many is *Treasure: From Tragedy to Trans Justice: Mapping a Detroit Story* about Shelley Hilliard, a murdered Black trans teenager. I had the honor of screening that film for the Hiphop Literacies Conference at Ohio State University in 2016. She co-founded the New York chapter of the Malcolm X Grassroots Movement. A by-product of that was her film *Black August*. This film centered Hiphop performers and music to school their peers to the plight of incarcerated Black political prisoners (Rausch). *We Demand Justice for Renisha McBride* highlighted the consequences of suburban segregated sunset towns. The case in point demonstrated the dehumanization of a car-wrecked Black teenaged girl in Dearborn Heights, Michigan, in 2013. A white man shot and killed this girl for knocking on his door for help. The 2018 documentary

---

19. https://en.wikipedia.org/wiki/Dream_Hampton

It's a Hard Truth, Ain't It chronicled 13 incarcerated men as they studied filmmaking to explore how they ended up with decades-long prison terms. Another executive produced docu-series, 2019's *Finding Justice*, moves the lens from mass incarceration to mass criminalization of Black folks and our search for justice. For this work and much more, activist artist dream hampton was named one of the most influential people by *Time* in 2019.[20] This recognition came in the year she produced the documentary, *Surviving R. Kelly*.

Surviving was the documentary that did what the viral tape of R. Kelly "having sex with" and urinating in an underage girl's mouth in the early 2000's could not do. This documentary did what approximately $200,000.00 in civil settlements paid by R. Kelly to cover-up wrongdoings over the past two decades could not do. This documentary did what 25 years of journalism and careful research by Jim DeRogatis was not able to do. None of this got the courts interested in charging R&B/Hiphop Soul star R. Kelly for his abuse and exploitation of Black and Brown women and girls. *Surviving* created public empathy for the survivors by creating a carefully informed and curated platform for the stories of survivors and their families. *Surviving* was aided by #MeToo, #TimesUp and the work of activist and grassroots organizers. Assata's Daughters, Black Lives Matter, BYP 100 are organizations whose work on different fronts helped to make a way for *Surviving*. A Long Walk Home is an organization dream hampton reached out to for its expertise in supporting sexually abused young girls. The organization provided pivotal support for survivors as they told their traumatic stories. #MuteRKelly was co-founded by Oronike Odeleye and Kenyette Tisha Barnes with the goal of interrupting R. Kelly's eco-system of handlers, employees, music sales, concerts, and other entities that sustained his world of sexual exploitation of Black and Brown women and girls (and boys).

> When Odeleye and Barnes formed #MuteRKelly in 2017, few people were listening to the accusers who had stepped forward to tell their stories. They went on a mission to literally stop people from playing R. Kelly's music, trying to get it removed from radio airwaves and streaming services. The two also worked to get Kelly's label, RCA, to end his contract and gave a platform to local grassroots organizations working with survivors. Their push led to the industry acknowledging Kelly's wrongdoings more seriously than ever before. It also created a runway for "Surviving R. Kelly," the 2020 docuseries that brought national attention to the singer's abuse. (Finley)

Surviving validated so much for me. In an interview about *Surviving* with *Democracy Now* in February 2019, dream hampton said something that gripped me: Many more women than the survivors who appeared on camera told her their stories off-camera. These women knew that they would be shamed, not believed, and dragged. At the 2016 Hiphop Literacies Conference: Black Women & Girls' Lives Matter one panel featured a presentation by Ronette Burkes, then warden of the Ohio State Reformatory for women. This one thing she said has also stuck with me. Upwards of 80% of the women in the prison were victims, manipulated by men. The ma-

---

20. https://en.wikipedia.org/wiki/Dream_Hampton.

jority of these women don't see themselves this way. This shows how deeply ingrained it is for Black women and girls to support Black men, even when it's to our own detriment. As a survivor of teenaged and young adult sex trafficking, it took me a long time to figure out that I was exploited—not by R. Kelly. I was exploited by 4 pimps from the ages of 13-24.

Black women and girls are among the most vulnerable people in this society, as Black men and boys are more often foregrounded as endangered, miseducated, mass incarcerated, ignored by public healthcare, exploited economically. However, Black women are the fastest growing incarcerated population (Kajstura), experience the biggest health disparities, and face economic oppression. From an intersectional standpoint, "Black women are subjected to high levels of racism, sexism, and discrimination at levels not experienced by Black men or White women." This is the foundation of health inequities (Chinn et al.; "Did You Know? The Plight of Black Girls & Women in America"). Further, Black-on-Black conflict, subordination of Black women and girls and homophobia are historically and currently rooted in racism, white heterosexual male supremacy, and capitalism. This shows how systems colluded to support R. Kelly's decades' long reign of sexual violence against Black and Brown women and girls in plain sight. A guilty verdict came down on R. Kelly in New York, September 27, 2021, for racketeering, sexual exploitation of children, forced labor and sex trafficking (Tsioulcas). Though, as of the writing of this piece, he still has more trials and charges to face in Illinois and Michigan:

> The rhetoric that allowed Kelly's pattern of abuse continued immediately after news broke. Outside the courtroom, Kelly's supporters blasted his music and cursed those "lying bitches." Twitter users called Aaliyah "fast" in the same breath they condemned Kelly. Bill Cosby, who was found guilty of aggravated indecent assault but was recently released from prison after his conviction was bizarrely overturned, said that Kelly was "railroaded" and didn't have a fair trial. (Finley)

R. Kelly's conviction is the manifestation of a herculean amount of labor, by so many mostly women organizers and allies, for such a long period of time; yet it seems miniscule in the face of the deep-seated hatred of Black women and girls that this case represents.

dream hampton represents an independent activist artist who has been able to produce culture and art reflective of her political commitments to humanize Black people. Her work represents a belief in people and insight into critical social justice possibilities in Hiphop literacies and movement for Black lives.

To maximize their profits, the corporate music industry promotes certain narratives and representations thereby controlling how Black people including Black women are represented to themselves and the larger public. As Nicole Rosseau explains, "the needs of the political economy determine Black women's position in the U.S. social structure," … "Black women are a unique laboring class within the racialized patriarchal structure of the United States," … "[S]ocial rhetoric is meaningfully constructed and manipulated as a tool of oppression." (452)

Given this context, what activism is possible for women Hiphop performers and producers? The present brief review of celebrity corporate artists as activists and independent activist artists, gives some idea. It was clear from the conversation with the girls in the afterschool club that some girls found Nicki Minaj's performance as pleasureable and appealing, while others saw it as negative. This divide among the girls is reflective of the Black rhetorical condition: desired, despised, (in)disposable. Amplification of social justice possibilities is necessary to inspire informed community work.

For the most part, corporate celebrity artist activists (such as Nicki Minaj and Cardi B) don't have as much room to experiment with activist stances they can perform inside the commodified space of Hiphop, if they remain with major music labels. To recognize their contributions as well as their complexities, it is equally important to look at the causes they support, the stands they take, and the ways they use their platforms. As an independent activist artist, Noname's activism is equally legible across her performances, music, and platform. As far as Hiphop generations go, dream hampton is an O.G., who has been able to consistently and explicitly direct her output to social change. As an independent activist artist and producer (writer and filmmaker), she leverages her status, relationships with individuals, organizations and movements to produce art and culture, to push narrative shifts. Noname is on this same path.

So much more investment and work is needed in our society to shift the narratives that make devaluation of Black women and girls' lives normal. These narratives are almost ubiquitous. And while all of this is going down, our mostly white conservative citizens are trying to stop schools from teaching the racist history and systems of our country that continue to harm people. They want to keep the masses docile, homophobic and aggressively racist, or unmotivated to fight for social change, while major conglomerates stay banked up at the expense of our misery.

Black women and girls are working on many fronts to heal ourselves and recover from the constant barrage of everyday violence we experience. From my perspective as an engaged Black woman community literacy scholar and Hiphop feminist literacies performance activist, I see it as imperative to read the world with and through Black women and girls' words and works to reveal our complexities, strategies and possibilities for social change.

Works Cited

Adams, Biba. Joy Reid Responds to Nicki Minaj Call Out: 'A Teachable Moment'. *theGrio*, 15 September 2021, https://thegrio.com/2021/09/15/joy-reid-responds-nicki-minaj-tweets-teachable-moment/.

Associated Press. "Nicki Minaj Pulls Out of Saudi Arabia Concert". *VOX*, 9 July 2019, https://www.voanews.com/a/arts-culture_nicki-minaj-pulls-out-saudi-arabia-concert/6171468.html

B, Cardi. Forward. "Is There Room for Someone Like Me?." *State of Emergency: How We Win in the Country We Built* by Tamika Mallory (as told to Ashley A. Coleman), Black Privilege Publishing, Atria, 2021, pp. xi-xiv.

Bailey, Moya. *Misogynoir Transformed: Black Women's Digital Resistance*. New York University Press, 2021.

Brown, Ruth Nicole. *Hear Our Truths: The Creative Potential of Black Girlhood*. University of Illinois Press, 2013.

Chinn, Juanita, J., et al. "Health Equity Among Black Women in the United States," *Journal of Women's Health*, February 2021, vol. 30, no. 2, pp. 212-219. doi: 10.1089/jwh.2020.8868. https://www.ncbi.nlm.nih.gov/pmc/articles/PMC8020496/

Davis, Angela. Forward. "Dearest Cardi B." *State of Emergency: How We Win in the Country We Built* by Tamika Mallory (as told to Ashley A. Coleman), Black Privilege Publishing, Atria,\ 2021, pp. xv-xxi.

Decker, Megan, et al. "45 Things You Didn't Know About Cardi B: Everything You need to Know About the No-filter Rapper." *Harper's Bazaar*, 28 June 2020. https://www.harpersbazaar.com/celebrity/latest/g20634894/cardi-b-trivia-facts/?slide=1

"Did You Know? The Plight of Black Girls & Women in America." *African American Policy Forum*, http://www.44bbdc6e-01a4-4a9a-88bc 731c6524888e.filesusr.com/ugd/62e126_54d4f5a4634047fe894ec2db240cb487.pdf.

Fields, Tanya Denise. "Dirty Business: The Messy Affair of Rejecting Shame." *You Are Your Best Thing: Vulnerability, Shame Resilience, and the Black Experience, an Anthology*, edited by Tarana Burke and Brené Brown, Random House, 2021, pp. 22-32.

Finley, Taryn. "How The Adultification of Black Girls Allowed R. Kelly's Decades of Abuse." *HuffPost: Black Voices*, 3 October, 2021, www.huffpost.com/entry/r-kelly-black-girls_n_6159dcfee4b099230d24a29e

Garza, Alicia. *The Purpose of Power: How We Come Together When We Fall Apart*. One World, 2020.

Halliday, Aria. "Envisioning Black Girl Futures: Nicki Minaj's Anaconda Feminism and New Understandings of Black Girl Sexuality in Popular Culture." *Departures in Critical Qualitative Research* 6, no. 3, 2017, pp. 65-77. doi: 10.1525/dcqr.2017.6.3.65.

hampton, dream. *Surviving R. Kelly*. Lifetime Movies. Showrunner, Executive Producer, Peabody Award winner dream hampton, 2019. https://peabodyawards.com/award-profile/surviving-r-kelly/

—. *It's a Hard Truth Ain't It*. HBO. Produced and Directed by dream hampton, February, 2019.

—. *Finding Justice*. BET. Produced and Directed by dream hampton, March, 2019. dreamhampton.com

—. *Treasure: From Tragedy to Trans Justice: Mapping a Detroit Story*. Produced and Directed by dream hampton. 2015. dreamhampton.com

—. *We Demand Justice for Renisha McBride*. Democracy Now. Produced and Directed by dream hampton, 2013. dreamhampton.com

—. *Black August Hip Hop Project*. Malcolm X Grassroots Movement. Produced and Directed by dream hampton, 2010. dreamhampton.com hooks, bell. "Selling Hot Pussy: Representations of Black Female Sexuality in the Cultural Marketplace." *Black Looks: Race and Representation*, South End Press, 1992.

Juzwiak, Rich. "Nicki Minaj's Vaxx Flap Is Distracting You From Her Husband's Legal Issues." *Jezebel*, 16 September 2021, https://jezebel.com/nicki-minajs-vaxx-flap-is-distracting-you-from-her-husb-1847687597

Kaba, Mariame. *We Do This 'Til We Free Us: Abolitionist Organizng and Transforming Justice*. Haymarket Books, 2021.

Kajstura, Aleks. "Women's Mass Incarceration: The Whole Pie." *Prison Policy Initiative*, 29 October 2019, https://www.prisonpolicy.org/reports/pie2019women.html.

Lane, Nikki. *The Black Queer Work of Ratchet: Race, Gender, Sexuality, and The Anti-Politics of Respectability*. Palgrave Macmillan, 2020.

Lil Kim. *Hard Core*. Undeas Records, Big Beat, Atlantic Records, 1996.

Lindsey, Treva. "Let Me Blow Your Mind: Hip Hop Feminist Futures In Theory and Practice." *Urban Education*, vol. 50, no. 1, 2015, pp. 52-77.

Mayo, Kierna. Foreword. *She Begat This: 20 Years of the Miseducation of Lauryn Hill*, by Joan Morgan, Atria, 2018, pp. ix-xx.

Nicki Minaj. "Stupid Hoe." Cash Money Records, 2011.

Megan Thee Stallion. "OPINION – Megan Thee Stallion: Why I Speak Up for Black Women." *New York Times*, 13 October 2020, https://www.nytimes.com/2020/10/13/opinion/megan-thee-stallion-black-women.html.

Morgan, Joan. *When Chickenheads Come Home to Roost: A Hip Hop Feminist Breaks It Down*. Touchstone, 2000.

Murakawa, Naomi. Foreword. *We Do This 'Til We Free Us: Abolitionist Organizing and Transforming Justice* by Mariame Kaba, Haymarket Books, 2021, pp. xvii-xx.

Onley, Dawn. "Nicki Minaj's Brother Jelani Maraj Gets 25 Years to Life for Child Rape." *theGrio*, 27 January 2020, https://thegrio.com/2020/01/27/nicki-minajs-brotherjelani-maraj-gets-25-years-to-life-for-child-rape/

Painter, Nell Irvin. *Sojourner Truth: A Life, A Symbol*. Norton, 1997.

Rausch, Andrew. *I am Hip-Hop: Conversations on the Music and the Culture*. Scarecrow Press, Inc, 2011.

Richardson, Elaine. *Hiphop Literacies*. Routledge, 2006.

Rousseau, Nicole. "Social Rhetoric and the Construction of Black Motherhood." *Journal of Black Studies*, vol. 44, no. 5, Sage Publications, Inc., 2013, pp. 451–71, http://www.jstor.org/stable/24573096.

"See Her, Hear Her: Celebrating Women in Music," 8 March 2021, www.iheart.com/womensday/

Shange, Ntozake. *For Colored Girls Who Have Considered Suicide When the Rainbow Is Enuf: A Choreopoem*. Collier Books, 1989.

Taylor, Keeanga Yamahtta. "Succeeding While Black." *Boston Review: A Political and Literary Forum*, 10 March 2019, https://bostonreview.net/race/keeanga-yamahtta-taylor-succeeding-while-black.

Tinubu, Aramide. "Does Cardi B Have a High School Diploma?" *Showbiz CheatSheet*, 7 June 2020, https://www.cheatsheet.com/entertainment/cardi-b-have-a-high-school-diploma.html/

Tsioulcas, Anastasia. "R. Kelly Found Guilty of Racketeering and Sex Trafficking." *NPR*, 27 September 2021, https://www.npr.org/2021/09/27/1040528011/r-kelly-verdict-guilty-racketeering-sex-trafficking

Turman, Aiesha. *Black Girl Project*. Director, Aiesha Turman, Super Hussey Filmwork, 2010.

VanDerWerff, Emily. "The Taylor Swift and Nicki Minaj Twitter Feud, Explained." *Vox*, 22 July 2015, https://www.vox.com/2015/7/21/9012179/taylor-swift-nicki-minaj-twitter.

Watoto from the Nile "Letter to Nicki Minaj" (no longer available online or YouTube). Accessed 2012.

Williams, Sherri. "Cardi B: Love & Hip Hop's Unlikely Feminist Hero." *Feminist Media Studies*, vol. 17, no. 6, 2017, pp. 1114-1117. doi: 10.1080/14680777.2017.1380431

Author Bio

Elaine Richardson aka Dr. E is Professor of Literacy Studies at The Ohio State University, Columbus, where she teaches in the Department of Teaching and Learning. Her books include *African American Literacies* (Routledge, 2003), focusing on teaching writing from the point of view of African American Language and Literacy traditions, Hiphop Literacies (Routledge, 2006), a study of Hiphop language use as an extension of Black folk traditions, and *PHD (Po H# on Dope) to Ph.D.: How Education Saved My Life* (New City Community Press, 2013), an urban educational memoir that chronicles her life from drugs and the street life to the university. Richardson has also co-edited two volumes on African American rhetorical theory, *Understanding African American Rhetoric: Classical Origins to Contemporary Innovations* (Routledge, 2003) and *African American Rhetoric(s): Interdisciplinary Perspectives* (Southern Illinois UP, 2004), and one volume on *Hiphop Feminism—Home Girls Make Some Noise* (Parker Publishing, 2007). Her forthcoming book is titled *Reading the World with Black Girls*.

Higher Hussle: Nipsey's Post Hip Hop Literacies

Marquese McFerguson and Aisha Durham

Abstract

Nipsey Hussle is a post hip hop icon. In this essay, we mine popular music and media coverage of Nipsey to describe his artistry and advocacy anchored by his articulation of an African American diasporic identity, his ambivalence as an independent rapper within a mainstream music industry, and his leverage of Black capital in his Crenshaw community. We address these relationships—identity, industry, and community—to situate Nipsey within African American and hip hop literacies. By recalling relationships and roots, we call attention to emancipated blackness enacted by Nipsey Hussle.

Keywords

hip hop literacies, post hip hop generation, Nipsey Hussle, hip hop culture, diasporic identity

Nipsey Hussle is an East African West Coast native son. The Eritrean-American Grammy-winning Rollin' 60s Crip-come-rapper-activist was catapulted to global fame after collecting Crenshaw cred for mixtapes reminiscent of the South Central street-savvy, politically-grounded "real" rap that reigned a generation earlier. A Tupac for our time, Nipsey delivers poetic hood prophecies that inform post hip hop generation critical social justice possibilities (Perry). In this article, we mine lyrics and interviews from his music catalog and media coverage to describe his artistry and advocacy, which are anchored by (1) an explicit articulation of a Black gangsta and global or transnational identity (Richardson 13), (2) a claim to Black independence as a contracted rapper within a white-owned commercial music industry, and (3) a direct investment in Black capital by building a brand, clothing store, and a coworking space for his Crenshaw community. These publicly-available media discussions about his relationships with identity, industry, and community define Hussle's hip hop literacies (Richardson & Ragland). By recalling these relationships, we call attention to the higher hustle by the hip hop icon to embody and enact liberation or emancipated blackness.

Hussle represents the post hip hop generation. M.K. Asante defines post hip hop as a "now" period of sociopolitical transition when self-aware Black youth *stand against* the "minstrel toxins" marketed by multinational music conglomerates and *stand with* the previous hip hop generation to combat community concerns, such as racial profiling (Asante 5-7; Durham 254). Put plainly, Asante asserts his generation will no longer be "collectively identified by a genre of music that we don't even own"

(5). Hussle addresses the structural constraints of Black artistry in commercial media. He opts to remain an independent artist for much of his career in order to retain creative and economic control of his music and his brand by launching a record label, All Money In (Asghedom, "Nipsey Breaks Down Gang Culture"). Later, we return to Hussle's contentious relationship with the music industry to address how this stance attempts to defy the capitalist logic of blackness as a commodity.

In addition to his positions about community and commercial interests, Asante identifies the use of the term "post" as a generational construct that transcends music. He extends canonical research by Bakari Kitwana who distinguishes the hip hop generation from the white-oriented Generation X and demarcates it as a post-civil rights one for minoritized groups born between 1965-1984 (28-32). Hussle is part of the "post" generation grappling with the intensification of globalization, police militarization, mass incarceration, consecutive wars, economic instability, and job insecurity (Durham 254). Born in 1985, Hussle comes of age when West Coast-influenced (gangsta) hip hop dominates American popular culture and when a decades-long drug war is waged by California governor-turn-president Ronald Reagan. For example, mandatory minimum sentences for crack possession are introduced and harsher penalties for gang affiliation are redefined as "street terrorism" in California (Van Hofwegen). Local law enforcement amass federally-funded military-grade weaponry to launch unrelenting drug sweeps, busts, raids, and stings that place entire communities of color under siege. By 1990, the prison population dramatically increases in California with 23% of all African American men ages 20-29 cycling through some form of criminal justice supervision (e.g., prison, jail, probation, or parole) (Mauer and Huling 1). The popular perception and public policies shape the lived reality of Hussle and the post hip hop generation.

The lived reality of Black youth in South Central is repackaged as "real" rap in popular culture. It is a commodified celebration of drug-related street life that Asante suggests the "post" repudiates. Researchers addressing Black masculine scripts or gender performances have described the hard body or brash bravado in "real" rap as a strategic pose needed for street life survival (Jackson 70; McFerguson, "Outkasted Black Masculinity" 69; White 43). Lifting the public-facing mask, contemporary hip hop studies also explores the interiority of Black masculinity that includes expressions of self-doubt, stress, and anxiety (Forman 1-2; McFerguson, "Unveiling Our Scars" 79). Compton's Kendrick Lamar is an often-cited example (Chang). This search for deeper meaning animates the generational critique of gangsta hip hop in popular culture. It is important to note neither Lamar nor Hussle abandon "the real" wholesale. They work with it. Hussle, unapologetically references his gang association, which is sometimes noted by artists to gain respect and credibility in the rap industry (Gee). He is legible alongside prominent California predecessors (e.g., DJ Quik, MC Eiht, Eazy E, Kurupt, Snoop Dogg, Mack 10) and contemporaries (e.g., Game, YG 400, Jay Rock, ScHoolboy Q, Vince Staples). Still, he is also revered as an emcee for his ability to depict the fullness of Black life in the South Central District similar to filmmakers John Singleton (*Boyz n the Hood*) and Ryan Coogler (*Fruitvale Station*). Hussle's depictions sometimes rely on heterosexist homophobic hyperviolent language. Here, we might suggest Hussle rejects "the real fake" that he calls the "rap nigga" (Asghedom, "Rap Niggas"). The "rap nigga" is the media-manufactured gangsta minstrel defining Black men from the "post" generation. Instead, he rescripts the gangsta by lifting the mask and by identifying the structural conditions that produces him. In both interviews and lyrics, Hussle centers the devalued, dehumanized voices of his South Central community.

Hip Hop Literacies

The articulation of Black identity, independence in the industry, and investment in community exemplifies Hussle's hip hop literacies. Hip hop literacies are African-derived cultural practices developed by diasporic Black youth who manipulate, read, and produce language, gestures, and images to position and protect themselves in societies where they face public abandonment and precarious living conditions (Richardson and Pough 129; Richardson 2006, 43). Elaine Richardson situates hip hop literacies within broader Black ones, which are "based in the lived experiences of Black people and center the ways in which power and oppression operate in those experiences" (31). Hip hop literacies, in this way, are always already critical because they engage with power. Hip hop literacies serves as an important conceptual framework to understand the ways rappers perform and communicate culture, and it provides a critical lens to examine what Richardson describes as the interrelationship between performing products and performing authenticity and resistance in popular culture (12).

Street life is an important feature of hip hop popular culture where the gangsta—or the African adapted trickster turned "bad nigger" in the African American folk tradition—figures prominently in the underworld and the sonic lifeworld of Nipsey Hussle (Richardson 13). In ghettofabulous style, bawdy or lewd language, and hustle street consciousness, the gangsta challenges both race and class performances by defying codes of Black respectability and the conventions of Black subordination under white supremacy (White 43-44). At the same time when the dope-dealing gangsta functions as a race-class rebel, the figure can also conform to traditional American ethos of meritocracy and bootstrap capitalism. Hussle, whose rap persona recalls hard work, grinds inside the informal economy. It parallels, and in a way exposes, the violent, exploitative relations of the formal one in capitalism. Hussle harnesses the gangsta from street life to center his experience and others working outside or at the bottom of the capitalist economy (much like the California-founded Black Panther Party and Black Lives Matter movement that privilege the working class). He imagines radical change from the bottom upward. We reference gangsta similarly. Its popular and political iterations inform his relationship to identity, the music industry, and the Crenshaw community. We mark these as hip hop literacies that aim for a higher hustle of emancipated blackness.

Hussle's Hip hop Literacies: Identity, Industry, and Community Identity

Hussle's Black bicultural blood family and Rollin' 60s Crip gang family anchor his hip hop identity. Both identities are marginalized. In US race-based conversations, for example, Black American immigrant experiences are decentered (Celeste 3-4); and, in class-based conversations residents with gang reps are derided as social problems rather than potential problem solvers in the community. In a bell hooksian move, Hussle mines the marginal space as a productive place of identity formation that enables him to pivot across multiple points of difference. He reclaims the two identities to offer audiences transnational blackness and bottom-up "street consciousness" to reimagine Black belonging.

Crip Family. The transformation of the small-time hustle of an 11-year-old candyman-shoeshine boy into the big Hussle begins after he leaves his mother's home to join the Rollin' 60s Crip family (Berish). He joins the gang to adapt and survive street life. In the song, "Crenshaw and Slauson (True Story)," for example, Hussle shares a harrowing coming-of-age narrative about the hardness that has robbed him of his humanness, his childhood. He remembers being a kind-hearted, humorous, charismatic kid who smiled often until he had to deal with violent threats (from rival gangs and aggressive cops), extreme poverty, and the tragic deaths of close friends in the "mean streets" (Asghedom, "Crenshaw & Slauson"). It hardens him. "I was raised in South Central LA … As kids we come from nurturing, but there is a lack of that, and the coldness you get from going outside and having to survive. You get in survival mode," he told a Hot 97 radio host (Asghedom, "Nipsey Breaks Down Gang Culture"). It is violence—the violence of poverty, aggressive policing, and other gangs—that moves Hussle to join the Rollin' 60s Crips.

The Crips carry multiple origin stories. Before its gang reputation, Crips might have reflected parts of the Black Power Movement when groups like the Black Panther Party would regard the working class and lumpenproletariat (or so-called underclass) as vanguards of the revolution. Here, C.R.I.P. is an acronym for Community Revolution In Progress (Fremon). Another Crip origin story claims a group of teen boys banded together to protect themselves from other teen gangs in an increasingly violent Southern Los Angeles area (Williams). Both stories recall self-preservation and community protection as primary concerns for the creation of the Crips. These stories mirror the rapper who joins the gang for protection and who hustles in the formal and informal economy to preserve his community.

One way Hussle draws on his Crip identity as a rapper with street credibility is through his artistic collaborations that serve as a figurative olive branch to gang rivals. Together, the Pirus and Bloods are sworn enemies of the Crips. The decades-long bloodshed between the gangs is well documented (Peralta). Still, Hussle collaborates with The Game (Jayceon Taylor of Cedar Block Pirus), Jay Rock (Johnny McKinzie Jr. of Bounty Hunter Bloods), and YG (Keenon Jackson of Tree Top Pirus). The South Central rappers do more than drop verses over beats. His collaborations are invitations for Black men to see each other as brothers rather than rival gang members. This represents the political and cultural work—the higher Hussle—that he leverages to strengthen community.

Speaking to a Dallas based radio host who assumes he has left Rollin' 60s Crips, Hussle asserts:

> I'm not out the gang. You don't get out of a gang, truthfully. You just, you redirect your energy. I'm not a gang banger. [T]hat ain't nothing you gone ever put down. Because, if you ever put it down you never were a part of it for real. You don't just hang up your rag and say I'm not from this community no more. (Asghedom, "Nipsey Hussle Talks About What His Real Name Means")

Hussle refuses to disavow his Crenshaw community—including his fellow gang members who comprise it. Hussle uses his affiliation with the Crips to further extend that figurative olive branch to law enforcement. In a letter to members of the Los Angeles Police Department (LAPD), Hussle writes:

> Our goal is to work with the department to help improve communication, relationships and work towards changing the culture and dialogue between LAPD and the inner city. We want to hear about your new programs and your goals for the department as well as how we can help stop gang violence and help you help kids. (Madden and Carmichael)

The proposed Monday meeting with LAPD would have happened if it were not for Eric Holder who brutally murders Hussle a day earlier (Griffith). In the wake of Hussle's death, members of the LA Crips and Bloods discuss a cease-fire and a possible peace march. By Friday, once sworn enemies share a unity walk at the intersection of Crenshaw Boulevard and Slauson Avenue to honor the homegrown hip hop icon (Muhammad). Hussle offers us a "true story" to address violence—violence of extreme poverty, aggressive policing, and warring gang culture. On record and in real life, he uses his Crip family connection to stop violence, to broker peace.

Eritrean (African American) Family. Before his Hussle hip hop persona, Ermias Joseph Davidson Asghedom is a second-generation African immigrant child of an Eritrean father who flees war to settle in California in the 1980s. Throughout his childhood, Hussle learns about his East African heritage and as a teen takes a 3-month trip with his father to Eritrea where he connects with his African family and reconnects with African roots that shape his Black American identity (Jennings, "Nipsey Hussle had a Vision for South L.A."). Eritrea informs how Hussle considers coexistence as an African American and as a Rollin' 60s Crip to strengthen Black communities—local and transnational.

Returning to the Hot 97 interview, Hussle adds:

> It was profound going over there. It made a huge impact. I was different. There is me before I went and me after I came back ... I was still knee-deep in what was going on in LA when I came back, but I had a different ... [Hussle pauses.] You know you got those two voices. [He points to his shoulder.] This one became a lot louder. I couldn't fake like I wasn't exposed to the way

things could be … I couldn't just embrace the narrative of this is how this shit goes and it is what it is. That [gang violence] wasn't reality to me no more. (Asghedom, "Nipsey Breaks Down Gang Culture")

In both radio interviews Hussle provides critical reflection about his West Side Crip and East African blood families that anchor his bicoastal, bicultural Black identity. Hussle does disavow violence; he does not diss members of his Crenshaw community. Building on Richardson and Imani Perry who describe the gangsta and outlaw figures respectively, Regina Bradley suggests cultural and social outcasts draw from experiences of otherness in generative ways to offer counternarratives about blackness (12-13). Hussle rescripts the dominant narrative about the gangsta as disposable, deviant, and wholly unproductive by demonstrating his own civic and cultural engagement. Moreover, he uses his life story of cultural citizenship to rewrite African Americanness within a global context of transnational blackness (Celeste). In doing so, Hussle offers the post hip hop generation an Afropolitan identity that is neither class nor country bound (Neal 152-153). He engages in what Anima Adjepong describes as a Afropolitan project by fusing his immigrant-raised African-sense of Eritrean ethnicity with his diaspora-defined Black American racial identity (249). His full embrace of all folks who make up the Black community characterizes one of Hussle's hip hop literacies.

Industry

Independence or self-reliance marks the "self-made" Black rapper in relation to a largely white-owned music industry. Independence is a second example of Hussle's hip hop literacies. Hussle develops his street grind as a teen. First, he bikes, buses, and walks five hours to create beats and record music in a one-hour free Saturday summer course at the Watts Tower Art Center (Jennings, "Tens of Thousands Mourn Nipsey Hussle"). He applies his dogged commitment to making music to selling mixtapes from the trunk of his car. Hussle copies the entrepreneurism that he witnesses on Slauson Avenue where Muslim brothers sell incense and the independent newspaper, *The Final Call* (Berish). It is the buy-Black capitalism magnified in Eritrea that becomes the blueprint for building his music business success, which is seen in his creative production, community-centered content, and contractual labor within and against an exploitive industry.

Creative production. Hussle gains notoriety because of his mic skills but it is his marketing of self-produced mixtapes that makes the rapper renown. Before he drops an album, Hussle relies on his local fanbase to market his "brand" and his mixtapes. Mimicking multinational corporations like Nike under late or consumer capitalism, Hussle advertises his new album with limited copies on social media. For Hussle, limited supply builds demand. He controls its distribution to promote scarcity and imbues abstract meaning to justify the upcharge of $100 per copy. It works.

Addressing the Crenshaw album rollout in a radio interview, Nipsey said:

Normally, you distribute your hard copies to retail. You send them to Best Buy, Target, your mom and pops [stores], but we didn't have a deal. We were indie. So we didn't have a retail relationship. So, we printed up our own hard copies and did a popup shop in L.A. We did a limited amount ...

There is only a certain amount [of] J's [or Nike Jordan sneakers] they are gonna release. It's only gonna be a certain amount of pieces. And that got people sitting around the corner camping out and paying high for it ...

I realized its value in scarcity. Music is the opposite. If a billion people want it, a billion people can get it. But the hard copy version, imma do a thousand of these and sell them for a hundred dollars each. And I'm going to sign them and make them double down as a concert ticket. So, if you buy one of these hard copies, you can get into this concert that you can't buy tickets to. The first night in L.A. we sold the whole thousand. Jay Z bought 100 of them and the other 900 we sold at the popup shop. That opened my eyes to a lot as far as how we can approach the game different and be successful. (Asghedom, "Nipsey Hussle Talks Victory Lap")

The commercial success of the album fuels his desire to remain an independent artist. Unlike other aspiring young rappers who might cut a record deal to bank bonuses and company perks, Hussle's marketing suggests cutting the industry's "middleman" might maximize profits. His mixtapes and album sell without a major distributor. When he signs with Atlantic Records, Hussle retains ownership of his masters, which includes the legal right to license recordings to third parties to use in television shows, films, commercials, or sampled songs. He maintains his independence by retaining financial and creative control over his artistry.

Contractual labor. Contractual independence distinguishes Hussle from "rap niggas." In the song of the same phrase, he states "I own all the rights to all my raps, nigga," (Asghedom, "Rap Niggas"). Wordplay here works within and against capitalism. Capitalism develops from slavery when Black people are deemed property for white owners to extract unfettered labor without compensation. Capitalism hinges on slaveability or the ability to commodify both bodies and things through blackness (Smith 67). During the Jacksonian period, poor propertyless white people distinguish themselves from enslaved Black persons by asserting claims of ownership—ownership of their white bodies and white labor needed to enter contracts and later to vote (Ogbar 13). This race-class relationship, rooted in slavery, informs modern capitalism. Hussle calls attention to Black ownership at the same time he recalls blackness-as-commodity by deploying "nigga." He is not an owned rapper. Here, we might return to Richardson via Hussle who addresses hip hop as a negotiation between performing commodity (i.e., white-owned Black culture) and performing resistance (i.e., Black-owned Black culture). To be certain, music ownership does not guarantee Black radical politics. Independent label owner and convicted killer Suge Knight of Death Row Records is an example. Regardless, Hussle recognizes *a freedom* in owning his music—owning his Black self—in the music industry with the creation of his label All Money In (Asghedom, "Nipsey Breaks Down Gang Culture"). It is the economic freedom that translates to the creative and political empowerment for him and for members of the post hip hop generation.

Community-centered content. Hussle maintains creative freedom—marketing to a broader audience, remembering his Crenshaw roots. Mass appeal matters if Crenshaw comes. Hussle references the hyperlocal with album and song titles: Crenshaw, Slauson Boys I, Slauson Boys II, Fly Crippin, Blue Laces, and R.S.C for Life (Rollin Sixties Crip for Life) are examples. The street autoethnographer creates a sonic lifeworld in his mixtapes about the Crenshaw District. Hussle employs the African-derived collective-I or what Norman Denzin describes as the "universal singular" that mines a particular (Crenshaw) experience that is at once speaking to broader scenarios, stories, or struggles (268). Hussle provides an example by referencing the LA Lakers' Lebron James. "Lebron is from the hood. He from the struggle," Hussle said. "I think anyone who is a hip hop head and comes from the struggle, Nip Hussle is gonna be one of your favorite narratives and one of your favorite approaches to hip hop ... He fits who I'm speaking to" (Asghedom, "Rap Radar").

Hussle's hip hop literacies is characterized by his claim of independence—his claim to owning his Black body and Black body of work. Even as a contracted artist, he adopts an agentic stance in an industry that wills rappers to bend to the will of the market. Hussle resists becoming a commodity or an owned rapper. We mark this as a resistance within and against capitalism. More than rappers negotiating a record deal, Hussle invites Black people to recognize our worth and value—our Black capital—needed to build our communities.

Community

The refrain of community is echoed in all hip hop literacies. In music lyrics and media interviews, Hussle re-members his homeplace as a vibrant space where displaced, dispossessed people are rich in resilience and resourcefulness. The self-reliance he hones early on street corners and afterschool classes makes possible his "self-made" brand of hip hop entrepreneurism, which capitalizes his business investment for social change (Lombard 3; Madichie 169, 187). Hussle buys back his block. He buys two properties abandoned or devalued to create new space, new opportunities. The coworking space and clothing store extends Hussle's grassroots activism of paying forward by giving back. He is still brokering for people working above and under ground. Hussle's investments in Crenshaw properties are investments in Crenshaw people. We mark this form of Black capital, community investment, as the third articulation of Hussle hip hop literacies.

Coworking space. Hussle builds capital to reimagine his Crenshaw district. He partners with Black LA developer David Gross to build Vector90, which is a two-story property with private offices with coworking or shared spaces where entrepreneurs can grow their business without the big initial investment in property ownership (Gross). It is the first floor of Vector90 where Afrofuturity is concretized. The youth STEM (Science, Technology, Engineering, Math) program bridges California's inner city with Silicon

Valley. There, we might see an aerospace engineer Aisha Bowe or computer scientist Alan Emtage in the making. The youth program is called, Too Big to Fail (Kelley). It recalls the public bailout of private corporations to prevent economic collapse and widespread catastrophe. Hussle takes a similar approach to Black inner city youth with his time, energy, and capital (Ekpo). In the Crenshaw District where some people see blight Hussle sees possibility. *Source* Writer, Ime Ekpo, reports the program might be modeled in Atlanta, Baltimore, and Washington DC. Hussle banks on Black capital.

Marathon clothing store and brand. Coming full circle, Hussle buys a clothing store and launches a designer line in the same shopping center where he used to sell music in the parking lot. It would be his second attempt after police raids and his brother's prison sentence (Asghedom, "Nipsey Hussle's Journey"). Fashioning himself after Jay Z and Puff Daddy, Hussle adopts the FUBU branding for the Crenshaw community. Crenshaw *is* the brand. One of its most profitable items is a plain shirt with cursive type that reads: Crenshaw. Representing Crenshaw is not the cultural appropriation of Forever 21, which markets Compton cool with its "NWA, Straight Outta Compton" shirts to a largely white consumer base (Tefler). Marathon is based in the Crenshaw district and employs residents, some of whom with previous criminal records, that serves as a testament to his commitment to an inclusive community where all people have value and valued interests.

The name Marathon itself is significant to consider how he perceives himself and his Crenshaw community. He said Marathon represents:

> Endurance … It stands for staying down. It stands for not quitting and accepting the ups and downs of whatever game you commit yourself to and riding it out. Because that's the reality of greatness or success, it comes with a rollercoaster ride … To make that the basis of our fashion line, I look at it like we are honoring the people who ain't quit. We honor the people who stayed down. (Asghedom, "Nipsey Hussle's Journey")

The store opening, for Hussle, is not a sprint. It comes to represent a race he has run in community with resiliency. Two years later, Nipsey Hussle is murdered outside of the Marathon Clothing Store by Eric Holder, an assumed Rollin' 60s Crip gang member. "Nip put his heart and soul on Crenshaw and Slauson," his younger brother says at Hussle's funeral (Dalton). An Eritrean flag drapes the casket in a street of more than 20,000 mourners. Crenshaw and Slauson—the location of Marathon Clothing—is renamed Nipsey Hussle Square (Nissen). "The marathon continues," is their rally cry for a community and a generation.

Conclusion: Homerun

In this article, we pointed to the Higher Hussle—the bigger than hip hop literacies as critical social justice possibilities of freedom that Nipsey rescripts from the bottom-up. In music lyrics and media coverage, he described Black identity as gangsta and global, independence as a Black artist with creative and financial control, and Black capital *in and with* the community where he brokered peace and literally built viable opportunities with Marathon and Vector90. We recognize these collectively as a form of emancipated blackness. When Hussle and his post hip hop generation contemporaries like Lamar dare to drop the mask to make room for different performances of masculinity, they provide permission for all of us to live out our full humanity.

We close by remembering Hussle and "Loaded Bases" (Asghedom). On the track from his debut studio album, Hussle lamented that the obstacles in the Crenshaw District should have blocked him from becoming a multimillion-dollar musician. They didn't. He "Willie Mays" them (Asghedom, "Loaded Bases"). With musical hits, Nipsey helped place Crenshaw players in better positions to win in life. The first base might have a Rollin' 60s Crips he employed at the Marathon clothing store, the second might have included a Crenshaw rapper signed to All Money In Records, and on third base there might have been a Too Big to Fail STEM kid encoding Afrofutures. The bases are loaded. Nipsey Hussle reminds us with Black solidarity, we are bound to win.

Ermias Asghedom you made it, home.

Works Cited

Adjepong, Anima. "Afropolitan Projects: African Immigrant Identities and Solidarities in the United States." *Ethnic and Racial Studies*, vol. 41, no. 2, 2018, pp. 248–66, doi:10.1080/01419870.2017.1281985.

Asante Jr, M. K. *It's Bigger Than Hip Hop: The Rise of the Post-Hip-Hop Generation*. Macmillan, 2018.

Asghedom, Ermias. "Crenshaw & Slauson." *Crenshaw*, All Money In No Money Out, Inc, 2013. *Spotify*, www.open.spotify.com/album/1C5gVWv1k7r0LxsrIL8OL8.

—. "Nipsey Hussle's Journey of Opening a Store in the Middle of His Hood in Crenshaw." *YouTube*, uploaded by World Star Hip Hop, 14 June 2017, www.youtube.com/watch?v=2FnFUCgo7x8.

—. "Nipsey Breaks Down Gang Culture." *YouTube*, uploaded by HOT 97, 22 February 2018, www.youtube.com/watch?v=XEgPVv_9_W8.

—. "Nipsey Hussle Talks About What His Real Name Means." *YouTube*, uploaded by 97.9 The Beat, 5 March 2018, www.youtube.com/watch?v=nomYSnSaXyA.

—. "Loaded Bases." *Victory Lap*, All Money In No Money Out and Atlantic Records, 2018. *Spotify*, www.open.spotify.com/album/6rcbbhcm8Os7EiVRHP9Aef.

—. "Rap Niggas." *Victory Lap*, All Money In No Money Out and Atlantic Records, 2018. *Spotify*, www.open.spotify.com/album/6rcbbhcm8Os7EiVRHP9Aef.

—. "Rap Radar." *YouTube*, uploaded by Tidal, 1 January 2018, www.youtube.com/watch?v=GVCNREwfGuM.

—. "Nipsey Hussle Talks Victory Lap." *YouTube*, uploaded 97.9 The Box, 1 April 2019, www.youtube.com/watch?v=HctuJBXkHys&t=361s.

Berish, Brett. "Self Made Tastes Better, Episode 7." *YouTube*, uploaded by Luc Belaire, 1 March 2018, www.youtube.com/watch?v=dJ6pgb4O6wA.

Bradley, Regina N. *Chronicling Stankonia: The Rise of the Hip Hop South*. University of North Carolina Press, 2021.

Celeste, Manoucheka. *Race, Gender, and Citizenship in the African Diaspora: Travelling Blackness*. Routledge/Taylor & Francis Group, 2017.

Chang, Jeff. "Kendrick Lamar And The Post-Hip-Hop Generation." *Buzzfeed*, www.buzzfeed.com/zentronix/kendrick-lamar-and-the-post-hip-hop-generation. Accessed 20 July 2021.

Gross, David. "Nipsey Hussle's Business Partner David Gross on Ownership." *YouTube*, uploaded by Complex News, 25 October 2019, www.youtube.com/watch?v=K-czYvcShW4.

Dalton, Andrew. "Nipsey Hussle Becomes Face of Downtown LA on Day of Memorial." *AP News*, 11 April 2019, apnews.com/article/80c767701269460687cc4016858d3ed9.

Denzin, N. K. "Performing [Auto] Ethnography Politically." *Review of Education, Pedagogy, and Cultural Studies*, vol. 25, no. 3, 2003, pp. 257-278. doi:10.1080/10714410390225894

Durham, Aisha. "_____ While Black: Millennial Race Play and the Post-Hip-Hop Generation." *Cultural Studies ↔ Critical Methodologies*, vol. 15, no. 4, 2015, pp. 253–259, doi:10.1177/1532708615578414.

Ekpo, Ime. "Nipsey Hussle Set to Launch STEM Programs in his Hometown of Crenshaw for the Youth." *The Source*, 8 February 2018, www.thesource.com/2018/02/08/nipsey-hussle-set-to-launch-stem-programs-in-his-hometown-of-crenshaw-for-the-youth/.

Forman, Murray. "'Things Done Changed': Recalibrating the Real in Hip-Hop." *Popular Music and Society*, vol. 44, no. 4, 2020, pp. 1–27, doi:10.1080/03007766.2020.1814628.

Fremon, Celeste. "Behind the Crips mythos." *Los Angeles Times*, 20 November 2007, www.latimes.com/archives/la-xpm-2007-nov-20-et-book20-story.html.

Gee, Andre. "How Tekashi 69 and Other Artists Highlight America's Trivialization of Gang Culture." *Uproxx*, 3 April 2018, www.uproxx.com/music/tekashi-trivialization-gang-culture-hip-hop/.

Griffith, Janelle. "Nipsey Hussle's Planned Meeting with L.A. Police." *NBC News*, 1 April 2019, www.nbcnews.com/news/us-news/nipsey-hussle-s-planned-meeting-l-police-gang-violence-go-n989676.

Jackson II, Ronald L. *Scripting the Black Masculine Body: Identity, Discourse, and Racial Politics in Popular Media*. State University of New York Press, 2006.

Jennings, Angel. "Tens of Thousands Mourn Nipsey Hussle." *Los Angeles Times*, 11 April 2019, www.latimes.com/local/lanow/la-me-ln-nipsey-hussle-funeral-memorial-staples-crenshaw-20190411-story.html.

Jennings, Angel. "Nipsey Hussle Had a Vision for South L.A." *Los Angeles Times*, 7 April 2019, www.latimes.com/local/lanow/la-me-nipsey-hussle-south-eritrea-south-los-angeles-20190407-story.html.

Kelley, Sonaiya. "With a New STEM Center and a Revolutionary Marketing Strategy, Nipsey Hussle is Music's Biggest Disruptor." *Los Angeles Times*,

16 March 2018. www.latimes.com/entertainment/movies/la-et-ms-nipsey-hussle-vector-90-victory-lap-.

Kitwana, Bakari. *The Hip Hop Generation: Young Blacks and the Crisis in African American Culture*, 1st ed. Basic Civitas Books, 2002.

Lombard, Kara-Jane. "Social Entrepreneurship in Youth Culture: Morganics, Russell Simmons and Emile 'XY?' Jansen." *Journal for Cultural Research*, vol. 16, no. 1, Routledge, 2012, pp. 1–20, doi:10.1080/14797585.2011.633833.

Madden, Sidney, & Carmichael, Rodney. "Caught in the System." *NPR*, 12 December 2020, www.npr.org/2020/12/12/945454343/caught-in-the-system-nipsey-hussle-lapd-.

Madichie, N. O. (2011). Marketing Senegal Through Hip-Hop - A Discourse Analysis of Akon's Music And Lyrics. Journal of Place Management and Development, vol. 4, no. 2, pp. 169-197. doi: http://dx.doi.org/10.1108/17538331111153179.

Mauer, Marc, & Huling, Tracy. "Young Black Americans and the Criminal Justice System: Five Years Later." *The Sentencing Project*, October 1995, www.sentencingproject.org/wp-content/uploads/2016/01/Young-Black-Americans-and-the-Criminal-Justice-System-Five-Years-Later.pdf.

McFerguson, Marquese L. "Unveiling Our Scars: Artist Statement." *The Review of Communication*, vol. 21, no. 1, Routledge, 2021, pp. 73–81, doi:10.1080/15358593.2021.1896024.

McFerguson, Marquese L. "Outkasted Black Masculinity." *Reimagining Black Masculinities*, edited by Mark Hopson & Mika'il Petin. Lexington Books, 2020, pp. 67-73.

Muhammad, Latifah. "L.A. Gangs Unite For March In Honor Of Nipsey Hussle." *Vibe*, 6 April 2019, www.vibe.com/news/entertainment/l-a-gangs-honor-nipsey-hussle-643140/#!.

Neal, Mark Anthony. "N*ggas in Paris: Hip-Hop in Exile." *Social Identities*, vol. 22, no. 2, Routledge, 2016, pp. 150–59, doi:10.1080/13504630.2015.1121571.

Nissen, Dano. "South L.A. Intersection to be Renamed after Nipsey Hussle." *Variety*, 9 April 2019, www.variety.com/2019/music/news/south-l-a-intersection-to-be-named-after-nipsey-hussle-1203185233/.

Ogbar, Jeffrey Ogbonna Green. *Hip-Hop Revolution : the Culture and Politics of Rap* . University Press of Kansas, 2007.

Peralta, Stacy, director. *Crips and Bloods: Made in America*. San Francisco, Calif: Independent Television Service, 2008.

Perry, Imani. *Prophets of the Hood : Politics and Poetics in Hip Hop* . Duke University Press, 2004.

Richardson, Elaine. *Hip Hop Literacies*. Routledge, 2006.

Richardson, Elaine. "Developing Critical Hip Hop Feminist Literacies: Centrality and Subversion of Sexuality in the Lives of Black Girls." *Equity & Excellence in Education*, vol. 46, no. 3, 2013, pp. 327–41.

Richardson, Elaine, and Alice Ragland. #Stay woke: The language and literacies of the #Black Lives Matter movement. *Community Literacy Journal*, vol. 12, no. 2, 2018, pp. 27-56.

Richardson, Elaine, and Gwendolyn Pough. "Hiphop Literacies and the Globalization of Black Popular Culture." *Social Identities*, vol. 22, no. 2, 2016, pp. 129–32.

Telfer, Tori. "Forever 21 is Offending People Yet Again." *Bustle*, 23 September 2013, www.bustle.com/articles/5562-forever-21-curator-of-all-things-compton-is-offending-people-yet-again.

van Hofwegen, Sara Lynn. "Unjust and Ineffective: A Critical Look at California's STEP Act." *Southern California Interdisciplinary Law Journal*, vol. 18, no. 3, 2009, pp. 679-702.

White, Miles. *From Jim Crow to Jay-Z : Race, Rap, and the Performance of Masculinity.* University of Illinois Press, 2011.

Williams, Stanley T. *Blue Rage, Black Redemption: A Memoir.* Simon and Schuster, 2007.

Author Bios

Dr. Marquese McFerguson is an Assistant Professor of Intercultural Communication within the School of Communication and Multimedia Studies at Florida Atlantic University. mmcferguson@fau.edu

Dr. Aisha Durham is an Associate Professor of Media and Communication in the Department of Communication at the University of South Florida. aishadurham@usf.edu

Free Your Mind and Your Practice Will Follow: Exploring Hip-Hop Habits of Mind as a Practice of Educational Freedom

Toby S. Jenkins

Abstract

In this article, I critically dissect hip-hop habits of mind as a professional way of thinking, being, and doing (knowing, speaking and behaving) and explain how these habits hold critical literacy and cultural literacy benefits for students and educators. The goal of this project was to identify and name hip-hop habits of mind and to explore how educators view them as professionally life-giving practices. In exploring the nature of hip-hop culture, themes such as freedom of thought, flexibility, truth-telling, creativity, authenticity, confidence, braggadocio, uninhibited voice, unrestricted movement, community, honor, integrity, and cultural efficacy were discussed and organized as the Hip-Hop Mindset framework. This framework consists of the habits, values, and practices that promote cultural efficacy and critical social action within hip-hop culture.

Keywords

Hip-hop habits of mind, ways of knowing, hip-hop values

Hip-hop education scholarship often explores how educators can better serve, reach, and engage students; more effectively teach students; and create educational environments that honor student cultures (Love "Anti-Black State Violence, Classroom Edition," *Hip Hop's Li'l Sistas Speak*; Petchauer; Emdin; Adjapong and Emdin; Kelly "Listening Differently"). This scholarship is significant and extremely impactful; however, additional hip-hop education scholarship situating educators, rather than students, in the center of change is needed. Understanding hip-hop not only as a pedagogical tool to "reach" students, but also as a professional mindset for educators expands the understanding of hip-hop's transformative capacity. Such scholarship explores critical questions about the focus and scope of social justice in education and contributes to the rich base of cultural asset and cultural wealth literature offering authentic, critical, and affirming literacies of traditionally minoritized cultures and communities (Yosso; Gonzalez et al.).

The goal of this project was to identify and name hip-hop habits of mind and to explore how educators whose work is centered in these habits view the habits as professionally life-giving. Hip-hop habits of mind are hip-hop educators' professional ways of thinking, being, and doing (knowing, speaking and behaving). In exploring the nature of hip-hop culture with hip-hop educators, habits of mind unfolded such as: freedom of thought, flexibility, truth-telling, creativity, authenticity, confidence, braggadocio, uninhibited voice, unrestricted movement, community, honor, integrity, and cultural efficacy. These habits hold critical literacy and cultural literacy benefits for both students and educators and are discussed in this article as the "Hip-Hop Mindset" framework. The Hip-Hop Mindset framework developed from research with hip-hop educators who narrated how they prepare students and approach, lead, and move in the profession. Taken together, these habits, values, and practices tpromote cultural efficacy and critical social action in hip-hop culture and schools.

Let Me Blow Your Mind: Hip Hop as Cultural Education

Hip-hop emerged as an academic field of study in the 1990s (Rose). The early years focused primarily on documenting the history of hip-hop music and understanding the larger pillars of the music culture (breakdancing, emceeing, djing, fashion, and knowledge of self). This scholarship was conducted primarily by historians and sociologists (Chang and Herc; Rose). The exploration of hip-hop culture in education began about 20 years ago with Greg Dimitriadis' publication of the first book-length ethnographic study of young people and their use of hip-hop culture, *Performing Identity/Performing Culture: Hip Hop as Text, Pedagogy, and Lived Practice*. A plethora of hip-hop education scholarship has followed, most of which has centered on the use of hip-hop in classrooms (Morrell; Stovall; Runell and Diaz; Emdin; Hill and Petchauer; Kelly "Listening Differently"; Kelly "I am not Jasmine; I am Aladdin"; Love *Hip Hop's Li'l Sistas Speak*; Petchauer; Endsley; Jenkins et al.; Richardson; Bradley). This scholarship has confirmed several positive learning outcomes of hip-hop in education: greater student engagement, increased caring about the subject matter, deeper personal commitment, greater levels of complex thinking, and higher personal development and learning impacts. Scholars also took up hip-hop as a topic of study, interrogating it as a venue through which oppressed people could interpret, resist, talk back, and reframe social language and understanding of their cultures.

Adjapong and Emdin note much of the existing research on hip-hop in education has focused on hip-hop based education (HHBE). Hip-hop based education has been written about since the early 2000s by scholars such as Marc Lamont Hill, Emery Petchauer, and others. Adjapong and Emdin draw their understanding of HHBE from collective work and explain it as incorporating hip-hop into school-based curricula through music and rhymes with the intent to teach subject matter. This practice often takes place in English Language Arts classes. Adjapong and Emdin distinguish hip-hop pedagogy from HHBE, explaining hip-hop pedagogy as the "art and science of using hip-hop as a teaching approach" (67). Petchauer also explains that the difference between HHBE and hip-hop pedagogy centers around hip-hop pedagogy's focus on the overall hip-hop aesthetic experience:

> As the most recent thread of scholarship on hip-hop, the aesthetic forms of hip-hop and their implications on learning and learning environments are ripe areas of research. Specifically, how can the habits of body and mind

within hip-hop support or harm educational goals and processes? Strangely, many researchers who recognize the damaging role that corporate media has had on hip-hop have been culturally irresponsive through the same practice: separating rap from the rest of hip-hop for the sake of analysis. Because hip-hop is conceptualized as a set of interrelated practices with common aesthetics such as sampling (Hoch, 2006; Potter, 1995; Shusterman, 2000), this line of research will hold more promise if researchers look at hip-hop holistically with practices in connection with one another rather than divorce them from one another. Studies that hold to this principle are better equipped to pinpoint the kinds of hip-hop pedagogies discussed above and the habits that educators might desire to cultivate in students. (965)

In this article, I do not focus on how to diversify the curriculum by including hip-hop as a genre of study, a method of knowledge acquisition, or a pedagogical approach. Rather, I explore hip-hop as a cultural way of being that impacts all aspects of how an educator or student participates, interacts, leads, and performs in any professional setting. Educational institutions from elementary through college, teach more than subjects. They also teach "ways of being." Through reward systems, discipline policies, institutional value statements/handbooks and verbal messages and cues, educational institutions clearly identify what is considered to be appropriate ways of thinking, behaving, and performing (for both students and educators). These standards are all influenced by societal ideals and cultures, which, as discussed earlier, are most typically white-normed. Broad cultural ideas about how being "professional," being "a good student," or being "well-behaved," are not normed on minoritized cultures, but rather on dominant ones. Even within important and valuable efforts to transform educational practices like school discipline policies, cultural hegemony can have wide influence. For example, in the use of social-emotional learning strategies (SEL), some experts find problems with defining and identifying "appropriate" behavior. Some scholars noted the "end-goal" often is steeped in white cultural norms of a good student being quiet, conforming, and cooperative (Caven 1). So even efforts to transform how minoritized students are treated in schools still fall prey to racist ideas about how a "successful" student should ultimately speak, act, or present.

Using community-created and derived cultures as not only an instructional tool, but also as a cultural mindset in education can be potentially transformative if educators authentically understand, value, and embrace these mindsets in their own lives. When educators understand hip-hop as a cultural mindset not determined by in/ability to rhyme, breakdance, or spin records, they can appreciate how everyone can benefit from a Hip-Hop Mindset. This appreciation does not involve copying hip-hop folkways; rather, the appreciation is about learning to consciously adopt ways to move through life boldly and culturally. Understanding hip-hop culture as a mindset requires educators to also understand the central and important function of criticality in hip-hop. The sense of urgency to say what needs to be said, do what needs to be done, and become who one dreams to become is strong within hip-hop. There is no time to wait, slow down, be mild, or mannered when trying to navigate through oppression.

Hip-hop culture and all of its elements (emceeing, djing, breakdancing, fashion, and knowledge of self) never were meant to be venues to help minoritized people conform and assimilate into larger society. The culture and its elements were created with the intent of being different, dancing differently, dressing differently, playing records backwards, and obtaining the knowledge of forbidden truths and histories (KRS-One 5). These concepts can be broadened to include generally having a different mindset, a different way of reading society and how to function in it. The messages and deeper forms of understanding derived from the perspectives, actions, and behaviors of hip-hop community members can be seen as a social justice possibility because they build cultural efficacy among communities that have historically been culturally miseducated. Educational researchers who have studied how students experience hip-hop cultural environments and programs have found these initiatives often strengthen student cultural efficacy [positive feelings about one's culture; strong understanding of the components, values, and structures of one's culture] (Jenkins *My Culture, My Color, My Self;* Love *Hip Hop's L'il Sisters Speak*, "Anti-Black State Violence"; Hill and Petchauer; Endsley).

Illuminating the importance of cultural education has become an important aspect of hip-hop research that connects its educational outcomes to other disciplines like ethnic and cultural studies. In the late nineteen-nineties, Manning Marable, a noted ethnic and historical studies scholar, offered an important explanation of the central role of culture in the lives of oppressed people:

> For the oppressed, the central and overriding question was one of identity: who are we as a people, what is our cultural heritage, what values or ideals can we share with other groups to enrich society as a whole, and what do we have a right to expect from the state and civil society? Within explorations of culture resides the kernel of an oppressed group's consciousness. (43)

A new vision of leading, teaching, knowledge production, and the physical parameters of campus is needed in education (Rautins and Ibrahim 24; Boyer 10). Based on extensive studies of first generation, low-income college students, Jehangir (15) suggests educational strategies such as the movement towards critical pedagogy (exploring race, class, gender and power); re-constructionist multicultural education (transforming the whole of the educational process); and learning communities (collaborative and cooperative learning tied to a shared living experience) offer important inroads towards change. These educational frameworks are important in the way they focus on the content, structure, and purpose of education. Beyond educational programs that solely help students navigate the terrains of the school, these theories speak to helping students to navigate their sense of self, place, and social belonging both inside and outside of the educational institution. This type of learning not only illuminates the personal lived experience, but also provides a deeper understanding of the plight and circumstances facing their cultural community at large.

To live and know oppression and struggle is one thing, to be provided an opportunity to understand its roots, reasons it persists, and brainstorm possible solutions transforms one's lived experience into critical academic capital and cultural knowledge in the classroom. Students' opinions of themselves, their families, and their communities are influenced by the education they receive; and their ability to critically "read" (interpret, evaluate, and understand) both their cultural experience and the ways in which the larger society systematically manipulates their experiences, can be sharpened in critically dynamic classrooms.

In the book, *Hear Our Truths: The Creative Potential of Black Girlhood*, Ruth Nicole Brown documents and analyzes her community-based work with Black girls. Brown intentionally and explicitly centers the voices of the girls in the research project (their poetry, music, stories, and conversations) to help readers understand how Black girls experience, understand, and make sense of their lived experience. By sharing their critical reflections on social issues, their community experiences, and their cultural histories, Brown clearly illustrates the intellectual gifts of the youth who participate in the program, "Saving Our Lives, Hear Our Truths" (SOLHOT). One of the most enduring messages in the book is its demand for educators to embrace the importance of collective memory within educational settings. In this case, collective memory involves creating learning experiences that encourage students to remember their histories and life experiences and educators to remember their past experiences with girlhood or boyhood. This concept is applicable beyond this one initiative and can relate to the teaching of culture, race, gender, class, or social justice in the classroom. Making time to remember all of our histories and experiences, and to critically reflect on how these memories, cultural wisdoms, and ways of knowing intersect with the present world can be an important form of critical literacy development.

Research Background

In "Framing and Reviewing Hip-Hop Educational Research," Petchauer categorizes hip-hop research into three strands of *focus:* hip-hop education (hip-hop in classroom practice or curricula); hip-hop identities (how youth identity development intersects with hip-hop educational experiences); and hip-hop aesthetic forms ("ways of doing or habits of mind"). The current project falls in the hip-hop aesthetic form strand as the goal was to pull together a framework of the Hip-Hop Mindset. Petchauer offers examples from his research to better explain what hip-hop aesthetics actually looks like in practice:

> . . . conceptualizing hip-hop not as a text to be analyzed or included in a curriculum but rather as a set of aesthetic practices containing and producing situated ways of doing (and being) constitutes a third strand in the literature . . . For one participant, sampling from various news sources and different classes to complete assignments was "in the spirit of hip-hop." Other participants consciously sampled the experiences of other students and friends to conceptualize education and navigate institutions, which is a form of sampled consciousness (Karimi, 2006). The study also illustrated how some hip-hop collegians navigated educational institutions that they saw as part of a hegemonic system that could compromise some of their ideals that were derived from hip-hop. These ideals included a graffiti-derived belief that one

should not have to spend money to create art and a rap-derived critical consciousness (Freire, 2002) according to which participants questioned meta-narratives and viewed institutions of higher education as containing insufficient representations of knowledge and the world. (961)

At the heart of my epistemological ambitions in this work is the desire to better understand and honor the ways of knowing, being, and doing found in many hip-hop communities. Achieving this understanding is a difficult task because it is almost impossible to demonstrate absolute cause and affect between how one thinks, how they approach practice, and their involvement in hip-hop (Petchauer 948). The reality is people flow in and out of various communities and experiences. To tease out whether observations of attitudes, actions, and approaches is a Black or Latinx American hip-hop cultural legacy, a deeper rooted African cultural legacy, or just a personality characteristic is challenging. Therefore, I do not attempt to make such a call. I unapologetically defer to the voices of the hip-hop community.

Ijeoma Oluo's words concerning acknowledging issues of race are relevant when exploring the presence of a phenomenon and its influence on a situation or person. Olua notes:

> It is about race if a person of color thinks it's about race ... Our lived experiences shape us, how we interact with the world. And how we live in the world. And our experiences are valid. Because we do not experience the world with only part of ourselves, we cannot leave our racial identity at the door. And so, if a person of color says that something is about race, it is—because regardless of the details, regardless of whether or not you can connect the dots from the outside, their racial identity is a part of them and it is interacting with the situation. (15)

Following Oluo's (5) logic, I rely on the voices of the hip-hop community because their identity within the community is part of them. In this case, these behaviors and ideologies I define as a "Hip-Hop Mindset" can be attributed to hip-hop if those who experience it interpret it as hip-hop. If the participants in this project assign hip-hop to part of their identity, then it is hip-hop because they are feeling or sensing an interaction occurring between their behavior, attitudes, thoughts, or values and their identity within hip-hop culture. Participants could have easily attributed their actions and behaviors to just being a part of their personality, "That's just who I am. I am a confident person." However, when asked, "How does hip-hop culture influence how you show up in the world?" participants responded with characteristics like "being bold" "having confidence" and "valuing creativity". These responses suggest participants link various experiences, histories, and concrete memories centered in hip-hop participation to how and why they now embody those characteristics as professionals.

Methodology

As a result of choosing to place a heavy weight on the voice of participants, I used portraiture to drive the overall methodological approach for this project (Lawrence-Lightfoot and Davis). Portraiture combines science and art to paint a holistic picture of an experience or phenomenon. It shares in the traditions and values of phenomenology, but it expands the boundaries of the methodology by combining empirical and aesthetic description in its focus on the convergence of narrative and analysis and in its explicit recognition of the use of self as the primary research instrument for documenting and interpreting the perspectives and experiences of the people and the cultures being studied (Lawrence-Lightfoot and Davis). Sara Lawrence-Lightfoot, the creator of this method of inquiry, offers the following description:

> Portraiture is a method of qualitative research that blurs the boundaries of aesthetics and empiricism in an effort to capture the complexity, dynamics, and subtlety of human experience and organizational life. Portraits seek to record and interpret the perspectives and experiences of the people they are studying, documenting their voices and their visions, their authority, knowledge, and wisdom. (5)

The value portraiture places on an interdisciplinary approach to research, in many ways, is also a value for the idea of the holistic researcher as portraiture allows a researcher to integrate all of their personal and professional interests, talents, and modes of expression into the work. In this regard, as a researcher, I am able to more fully present how I view and analyze the world as an educator, arts administrator, and hip-hop cultural group member. As an artistic methodological form, portraiture demands the researcher cross those boundaries that often separate the researcher from the subject matter and breakdown other boundaries that constrain research into strict, limited concepts of "rigor."

Portraiture places value on the authenticity of the research rather than issues of validity or reliability. The researcher's aim is to authentically represent the experiences, lives, and stories shared by the participants in the study. Whether or not multiple audiences will share the same experience is not a concern. Portraiture affirms every lived experience matters and offers us insight. Another critical component of portraiture is its focus on goodness. A propensity towards goodness does not mean portraits must only focus on positive aspects of a topic, nor does it mean information must be presented in a positive light. Rather, goodness refers to the refusal to be driven by past research tendencies to focus on failure and deficiency. Much research on ethnically diverse students is dominated by pathology. Some of my own early research also followed this path: what are the problems, what practices don't work, what alienates students, why students leave. Within the realm of hip-hop research, much of the scholarship is generally positive and affirming, but hip-hop is not yet viewed as such in the larger society. Broader societal opinions of hip-hop often are negative and deficit driven, as shared by the educators interviewed in this project. In my many years of writing about hip-hop culture, there is always a push back to include criticisms of the music, videos and lyrics. While it is important to have full, balanced discussions of hip-hop that communicate both the love for and criticisms of the music; it is also important to allow the culture to be more than beats and rhymes. The rich layers of the culture shaped by the hip-hop community provide access for people to experience hip-hop culture through poetry, art, dance, film, non-profit management experiences, etc. Critically dissecting and analyzing these layers does not always require a discussion about music lyrics. Therefore, portraiture is best suited for this study as it shifts the focus to discovering the inherent good in the people, institutions, or concepts studied and explores how the people who experience the phenomenon (hip-hop culture) define or interpret goodness.

Data Collection and Analysis

The conclusions at the core of this project are interwoven and centered in data collection and analysis across three studies.

In Study 1, I explored how young adults defined culture and viewed its utility in their lives (Jenkins *My Culture, My Color, My Self*). This study involved the analysis of semi-structured group and individual interviews with 153 college students across four states and an analysis of their accompanying "cultural self-portraits." Cultural self-portraits were short narrative, life-writing pieces outlining participants' cultural stories. Overwhelmingly, hip-hop was a part of the story many young adults told of their lives.

In Study 2, I focused on hip-hip environments (Jenkins "A Beautiful Mind"). This study was an immersive study of places outside of traditional educational institutions that convened or curated hip-hop experiences. My goal was to observe hip-hop educational environments to better understand the aspects of the culture that were so engaging to youth and young adults (and its implications for educational institutions). This collective case study included extensive time completing community-based observations coupled with semi-structured group interviews (Jenkins "A Beautiful Mind").

In Study 3, the current project, I began with the intent of pulling together my previous articles, books, and experiences with hip-hop in order to generate new understanding from collective work. Beyond my time as an academic researcher and professor, I spent a decade as an arts administrator and cultural curator. As a university cultural center director, I planned many hip-hop events from large-scale 20,000-person audience concerts, to academic hip-hop symposiums, to intimate spoken word lounges. So, I also bring a lens to the work as a cultural curator, which is important because I cannot forget what I have seen while in that role. As a cultural curator, I worked with young adults (hip-hop lovers); rappers, poets, dancers (hip-hop artists); managers (hip-hop executives); and researchers/writers (hip-hop scholars). The commonalities I have seen across these groups also drives my interest in better understanding their shared habits of mind. To ensure a contemporary read of the topic, I added new forms of data and information. I conducted a new literature review, particularly focusing on books written by hip-hop artists. I also analyzed series-length hip-hop documentaries (for access to the perspectives of major artists who I could not interview). I conducted a lyrical analysis of 40 hip-hop songs to map hip-hop language to beliefs, perspectives, and values. Finally, I conducted semi-structured individual interviews with 15 hip-hop educators and scholars-educators who are prominently known for their work in hip-hop. Purposive sampling was used to identify and contact educators who have garnered public recognition for their work and have specifically aligned their professional practice with hip-hop culture. Each interviewee was provided an opportunity to revise, restate, and re-check their final interview to ensure accuracy and authenticity (member check).

The Hip-Hop Mindset

Hip-hop culture has been documented and understood to be more than just the music that frames its foundation. The populations of people who identify with this culture and comprise what has now become multiple generations of hip-hop are also made up of more than artists. Hip-hop culture is embedded in the professional acumen of educators, community leaders, and various other professionals, all of whom make up the hip-hop community. Through the research that informed this project, nine hip-hop driven values, beliefs, attitudes, and behaviors emerged. I refer to these themes as "practices." A practice is defined as, "a way of doing something" or "the application of an idea or belief" (Merriam-Webster). These clusters and practices, which form the Hip-Hop Mindset Framework are organized below in Table 1.

Table 1
The Hip-Hop Mindset Framework

Mindset Cluster	Approach
Practice 1	Authenticity/Integrity
Practice 2	Creativity/Originality
Practice 3	Ingenuity/Cultural Efficacy
Mindset Cluster	**Drive**
Practice 4	Hunger
Practice 5	Competitiveness
Practice 6	Honor
Mindset Cluster	**Posture**
Practice 7	Confidence
Practice 8	Claiming Space
Practice 9	Commanding Attention

Approach

The first mindset cluster is approach. Approach involves three practices: (1) Authenticity/Integrity, (2) Creativity, and (3) Ingenuity/Cultural Efficacy.

Authenticity/Integrity: Authenticity/Integrity concerns representing oneself or community in a way that is real, clear and true. Hip-hop communities hold cultural group members accountable and expect them to show up as their full selves, not a watered-down version to please others. Authenticity emerging as a theme was not a surprise. I vividly remember how heavy the pressure to "represent" was when I was growing up as a teen in the late eighties. Michael Benitez, Vice President for Diversity & Inclusion at Metropolitan State University of Denver, explains how authenticity continues to hold relevance for him in his current professional life:

> When I see people lean on assimilation, lean on losing oneself to get opportunity, that often signifies a willingness to throw others under the bus. [It means they don't value] solidarity and looking out for one another, which results in individual interest as opposed to collective effort. Assimilation isn't an individual act. You have to throw shade on your whole community to assimilate. So, that means your colleagues, staff members, students who identify with your culture or race. When you deny yourself, you are also denying all of them. They get sacrificed and thrown under bus in the process.

Hip-hop's emphasis on authenticity is an important act of racial liberation. In so many spaces, ethnically diverse communities are pushed, harassed, and bullied into being something other than themselves. Willian Bowles, a high school teacher in South Carolina, offers personal insight:

> I believe in not being apologetic for who I am. I am at a school where I'm like one of three African American males there. I am not apologetic for who I am because they accept everybody else's normal. So, I be who I am. I be who I am and I dare somebody to say something about it. It's a way that they need to see us. You need to see me live and in color. So, students can know that it's okay to be themselves. I use African American language everywhere in my classroom. I let my students know that I speak African-American language and by doing that I am saying to them, "I want you to be who you are." I need them to feel comfortable with me and I need them to feel comfortable with themselves. And the only way that we can feel comfortable with each other is if we could communicate effectively-not in a foreign language that makes us feel less than.

The culture of authenticity within hip-hop can be appreciated not so much as a *pressure* to keep it real, but rather a *permission* to keep it real: to claim the community; to honor one's mother tongue; to be loyal to the crew; to name one's experience; and to speak one's truth. For people who do not identify with the music or culture, cultural authenticity may not be connected to hip-hop. As shared earlier, the Hip-Hop Mindset is not about copying hip-hop behaviors. Rather, the Hip-Hop Mindset is beneficial simply by how it gives a person the permission to be themselves. *Authenticity/Integrity* is a Hip-Hop Mindset that can be adopted, regardless of whether a person identifies with the culture. Hip-hop culture is on the other side of racial assimilation. It does not gently nudge hip-hop community members to be authentic; it gives a sense of urgency the community demands accountability.

Creativity: For this project, I interviewed 15 elite hip-hop educators. According to the *Sage Dictionary of Social Research Methods* (Jupp 85), elite interviewing is the use of interviewing to study those at the top of any system whether its sport, academia, religion, etc. All of the professionals I interviewed have achieved various forms of success, whether it is personal freedom and accomplishment, recognition in the field, or a solid professional reputation. One of the first questions I asked each of them was, "How does hip-hop culture show up in your professional life?" All 15 participants talked about creativity. Many shared being original and/or unique is critical in hip-hop and a major goal in their own careers. There is a value for innovating—being able to transform or remix something old into something new. There is a popular saying that hip-hop is about flipping something out of nothing. However, a deep examination of what hip-hop communities have been able to create indicates this statement is not quite true. As Andre Perry, Senior Fellow at the Brookings Institute asserts, "Something doesn't come from nothing. The question is do you see value in what most people see as meager? Do you see utility in what others would disregard as useless?" (134). Some people are able to read their world (their community, their life experience, their family) differently. It is a different type of cultural literacy, a literacy of cultural abundance and resistance. The young people who created hip-hop did not look at their lives and see useless junk. They looked past society's negative labels and saw their own talents and skills and created their own opportunities. The creative mind in hip-hop could turn a piece of cardboard into a dance floor and a record player into a music instrument. Hip-hop minds are always working to stand out, to be different, and to contribute their own unique flavor. This is a different measure of successful practice than meeting the standards and effectively doing the same things others are doing.

Ingenuity/Cultural Efficacy: Ingenuity concerns being clever and inventive. It is tied to the idea of cultural efficacy because before young people can develop inventions, they first must believe in their ingenuity and culture. As shared earlier, cultural efficacy is an optimistic belief in, appreciation for and respect of one's culture and the people in it (Jenkins *My Culture, My Color, My Self* 58). So many formal institutions within American society (education system, criminal justice system, religious institutions, etc.) continue to teach racially minoritized communities they are not enough. Hip-hop culture responds not by shrinking away in self-doubt, but by amplifying hip-hop communities' cultural ways of being and doing. When society's intellectual production (books, media, educational curricula) devalued Black and Brown voices, the hip-hop community answered by creating a movement wherein young people embody all the qualities society hated in them. Hip-hop took neighborhoods that had been economically destroyed by racist redlining and business development practices and transformed them into famous cultural landmarks in the public imagination.

Housing projects like the Marcy Houses and Queensbridge Houses were not spaces of shame because rappers claimed these communities as home, giving a sense of cultural pride to those who lived there. The hip-hop cultural response to a society that portrayed Black and Brown youth as unintelligent was to get paid millions of dollars for a career that required them to write and speak. Hip-hop artists do not whisper their thoughts; they project their voice and scream their emotions at society. A Hip-

Hop Mindset means not depleting one's cultural joy or shrinking away from telling the truth to fit in within white cultural spaces.

Educators with a Hip-Hop Mindset give themselves permission to do what is just and right. Educators should not have to ask permission to fight something like racism. Hip-hop culture reminds educators of their strength, endurance, and ingenuity and pushes them to invent unique paths, find new ways to view obstacles, create change and new strategies of resistance; and remain committed to their students, cultures, and communities. When I asked interview participants for one word that best described hip-hop culture, Bettina Love answered indomitable. "You can try to knock us out, baby, but we have an indomitable spirit. You can come with all you've got to trip us up. We're still going to figure it out. Ingenuity to the core."

Drive

The second mindset cluster is drive. Drive involves three practices: (1) Hunger, (2) Competitiveness, and (3) Honor & Kinship.

Hunger: People can be hungry for a lot of things—hungry for job opportunities, hungry for social change, hungry to make a difference, hungry to make a mark in the world. Hunger in hip-hop is about being very keenly aware of an opportunity, to work hard for the opportunity, and to acknowledge one's shine while doing great things. It is important to stress the word hunger brings with it particularly important sensibilities. Describing someone as hungry calls forth a different impression than describing someone as motivated. There is a sense of urgency that comes with hunger. A person who is motivated to eat might wait in line, a person who is hungry or starving might cause a scene. Andre Perry explains it perfectly:

> There's a level of hunger that I think is quintessentially hip-hop. I want it like a hungry rapper. I want to get on. I think that's a universal feeling of "wanting to get on." All kinds of people know what it is to seek opportunity. But that idea was introduced to me largely through hip-hop. There is this intense desire to get an opportunity—to get on the stage, to get a record deal, to get in a magazine, to be known and to be recognized. And it's not just for the fame, but to literally be seen and heard. It's about having a level of importance and impact. It can come off as being ambitious, braggadocios or even flamboyant at times. But if you're in hip-hop, you know, that's what we are all searching for, validation, each and every one of us.

Whether it is through the lyrics penned by artists, the curricula created by educators, or the community programs developed by nonprofit leaders, hip-hop community members are acknowledging young people are ambitious, skilled, talented, and intelligent. Similarly, education systems need to acknowledge and recognize different forms of academic and professional ambition and performance. Too often education systems want students to study subject matter the system chooses, participate in activities the system creates, achieve standards the system sets, and meet these goals while following rules of conduct and behavior the system establishes. Often these rules of conduct privilege cultures of quiet. But what if one's ethnic culture is not quiet? What if the process of working, achieving, and grinding is an active, lively, vocal, and energetic experience in the cultural community? Consider the difference between a lively family dinner gathering and a quiet, structured formal dinner. Just because a person is too uncomfortable to eat in certain settings does not mean they are not hungry. Educational settings can feel restrictive for both students and educators. Superintendent Baron Davis affirms the need to push against cultures that restrict bold ways of being:

> Hip-hop's history gives you the sense that in order for you to be heard, you've got to be loud. I'm a superintendent. So of course, I know there are a lot of spaces where young people are told not to be loud. But hip-hop gives me a different, philosophical understanding of loudness. When you play your hip-hop music, it doesn't sound the same when it's low. It doesn't have the same energy when it's played low. It has to have a certain decimal level in order for it to even sound right. So that's how I feel professionally. Sometimes you've got to have a boldness about your work.

How might educators achieve if they were allowed to let loose and be culturally free without being viewed as too much—too loud, too rowdy, too active? Crystal Endsley, Associate Professor of Africana Studies at John Jay College of Criminal Justice shares:

> Hip-hop taught me that it's okay to be a lot. I get called "intense" sometimes . . . I think of Missy [Elliott] and how she's fearless. She is fearless with it. She's so secure in who she is or at least she presents that way. Growing up watching her, I was like—oh, okay, this is a way to move in the world. Just extra bold.

Hip-hop community members want to feel totally and completely alive throughout the entire process—setting the goal, working towards the goal, and achieving the goal. This aliveness requires the field of education to make space for the vivacious, expressive, lively, energetic, hungry spirit that has always been a part of African cultural sensibilities (Boutte et al.; Boutte "And How Are the Children?"; Asante; King).

A vivacious classroom allows the freedom and flexibility for a noisier environment, for students to speak in their mother tongue or cultural language, and for participation to be unrehearsed, uncoordinated, and extemporaneous. In his work focused on "ratchetdemics," Christopher Emdin (as cited by Bump) offers an idea of what such a vivacious classroom experience might look like:

> Black and brown students who may be loud, or who may speak in slang and colloquialisms and relate more to hip hop than Hemingway, are taught from an early age that their "ratchet selves from the 'hood" must be opposed to their academic, intellectual selves, he said. ('Ratchet' is a hip-hop term derived from wretched that can mean loud, nasty or cool among other things, depending on context.) … It's a theory Emdin, a self-proclaimed "ratchademic," calls "Reality Pedagogy" and in it he asks educators of black children

to consider adopting the style of the preacher in a black church — playful and soulful, with a tendency toward rhyme, storytelling and call-and-response (can I get an amen?). (Bump)

Competitiveness: Having high expectations and ambition to be the best is probably viewed as a core value at most schools and colleges. The question here is do those high expectations extend all students? Do those high expectations extend to all faculty? Are there high expectations of and a bright future expected of a first year, Latino male instructor? Is he allowed to pursue his own ambitions, in his own way? I ask these questions because his cultural path to blazing trails as a new educator might mean he brings a countenance thick with swag into the school building. Can he do that, or must he be mild and meek in order to be accepted?

The spirit of competition in a hip-hop cypher is simultaneously intense, intimidating, nerve-racking, exciting, inspiring, and life-giving. Participants walk away from the space not bruised or defeated, but hyped, joyful, happy, and determined to crush it next time, even if they messed up. Healthy competition is a great thing, but most professional institutions have not mastered the art of creating spaces for healthy competition. Yet, these spaces exist in hip-hop communities. In hip-hop cyphers, young people demonstrate how healthy competition gives them life. The competition gives them reasons to get better or to get up in the morning. It gives them a reason to come back into the space. Also, hip-hop culture helps educators see both they and their students need to feel the fire of competition and stop running away from it. The reality is everyone wants to be great—educators and students. However, a cultural shift is needed to allow our educational spaces to free, open and energetic, intense and competitive, and healthy to support the natural pursuit of greatness for all in the community. In some communities, "achievement" is not a quiet enterprise.

Honor & Kinship: Honor emerging as a Hip-Hop Mindset made me feel proud as a fan of the culture. Too often, hip-hop is painted as deviant and disrespectful. For ethics like generosity, respect, love and a welcoming spirit to emerge as essential practices within hip-hop culture is refreshing. Hip-hop has become such a global phenomenon because it attracts people to it rather than repelling people from it. Rather than making others outside of the culture feel limited or less than (not fresh, not cool, not dope, not down), hip-hop culture affirms the fresh, the cool, the dope, and the down for those in authentic proximity to hip-hop culture. Listeners feel fresh when vibing to a hip-hop song. The energy is contagious. Schools should adopt the honor and kinship promoted in hip-hop culture. Instead of making students feel self-conscious and less than with the implication that how they show up in school is not welcome (imposter syndrome), schools should affirm students' identities and cultures and encourage students and educators to celebrate their abilities.

One of the most basic ways to understand honor in hip-hop is through the concept of respecting the mic (and thus the person on it). Being a listener in a hip-hop community is an active process. Listening also requires one to be a supporter and an encourager and promotes honor and kinship in hip-hop communities. Crystal Leigh Endsley explains:

> I'm a spoken word artist and the stage, in general, taught me about confidence. But those hip-hop rich spaces also taught me how to be an audience member too. It taught me that when someone else is on stage and they do something really well, to applaud them. To have a generous attitude. In hip-hop "behaving properly" when I'm not the one on stage, means giving the other performer the claps and response they need to feel good. Because as a performer you feed off of that. What gives you life when you're on the stage is the audience reaction. So, when you sit in the audience, you try to give that energy to other performers. Don't hold it back, don't save it for later. Keep that energy and focus on the stage and in the audience. And that applies in a real hands on way to regular life. If anyone in your life does something well or someone's having a really hard time, you show them real, vocal support. In an open mic, if a poet stumbles on their words, it's the audience that claps back up their confidence and gets them to start again. We've got to be that for our friends [students, colleague, supervisees]—being able to really embody support for people.

Behaving properly pulls into the familial and community ethic also present in hip-hop culture. Many of the educators interviewed for this project noted the importance of impacting the community through their work. As Tony Keith Jr., an independent scholar and activist notes, "Hip-hop is about asking yourself how can I make this accessible, make it plain? Let's make sure that the knowledge matters to the community." Community matters in hip-hop because there is a recognition of kinship and a sense of belonging to each other. Michael Benitez notes, "When you think about it from a literal standpoint, hip-hop requires a community … you can't be the only one in the space. And the connectedness that happens when that community gathers—there's nothing like it." Hip-hop is the community life experience artists pull from to tell stories in their lyrics; it is the community's interests and passions that community organizers tap into when they create programs and interventions; it is the community's style and swagger designers pull from to create hip-hop fashion; it is the community's needs or experiences hip-hop scholars research and write to advance understanding and social change. The community is central to any form of hip-hop production. Therefore, researchers must explore whether the centrality of the community in the hearts and minds of educators. For Emery Petchauer, community is the foundation of his work:

> I try to create educational spaces where students can see themselves as participants in the community rather than approaching community members as a kind of transaction. So, what does this have to do with hip-hop? I know from my experiences in hip-hop that when resources and assets are better connected, that changes the conditions and allows for really dope stuff to happen that you couldn't have imagined.

To better understand what Petchauer means by the idea of approaching community as a transaction in education, consider how community service or social justice initiatives are often approached as assignments, projects, extra-curricular experiences, but not as the collective responsibility of the educators and students in the school. If social justice were approached as a collective responsibility and core outcome (not just an idea to be studied or a project to experience), then achieving that goal would permeate throughout the institution.

Community asset mapping (McKnight and Kretzmann; Kerka) has long been offered forth as a viable practice by which educational institutions can begin to identify, value and better understand the assets (in the form of skills, knowledge, and expertise) available within their surrounding community. Tapping the local community as guest lectures, visiting scholars, master teachers, artists in residence, leadership trainers, or sites for experiential education and professional development situates the community as a powerful resource to help transform the school, rather than as a victim in need of the school's assistance. Aysha Upchurch, Lecturer and Director of HipHopX at Harvard University, explains hip-hop culture is what centers her sense of humanity:

> Hip-hop also reminds me to believe in humanity—that humans actually want to gather together in love and in peace. I've been able to see people gathered. I've been gathered. I've gathered with people where there's no shared spoken tongue. We are all in a space together and while we can't even talk to each other, we can still vibe and feel each other. It helps me believe that evil is taught. In our natural state, we all want to two-step at the same time. So, it helps me remember that the rose-colored glasses that I want to wear, it's okay to put them on. I can believe in humanity. I've seen how hip-hop can bring us together. It reminds me to believe that humanity is not utterly unsalvageable. We want to gather and have joy and love.

Posture

The final mindset cluster is posture or one's presence within their professional space. The three practices related to posture are: (1) Confidence, (2) Claiming Space, and (3) Commanding Attention.

Confidence: Most often, confidence in hip-hop is interpreted as swag—an attitude of assuredness personified through the way a person presents or carries themselves. Edmund Adjapong, Assistant Professor of Education at Seton Hall University clearly sees how a Hip-Hop Mindset has influenced his beliefs and sense of professional confidence. A naturally quiet academic, embracing a braggadocious sense of self-worth has been the extra-support Adjapong needed to navigate culturally difficult spaces in higher education:

> I think hip-hop gives me kind of a bravado attitude ... In order to be successful as an academic and in order to be successful in hip-hop, you have to be confident. So, in many ways you really have to have high self-awareness. You have to be aware of your talents and what makes you special—that's the

confidence. If you don't know who you are, then the world can depict or perceive you as other. They can make even you believe you don't belong. Knowing who you are allows you to also know that you deserve to be here. I think that has helped me a lot in academia. It's been really useful when I'm navigating spaces where I'm the only Black person … or I'm the youngest person.

In his reflection, Adjapong describes how cultural confidence does more than promote achievement; it promotes functioning in intimidating spaces. Timothy Jones, independent scholar and community activist, explained the confidence he has inherited from hip-hop culture influences both his approach to work and ultimately his desire to keep working:

Some may view it as over-confidence, some may view it as arrogance, but one of the attitudes I get from hip-hop is knowing that I'm fearfully and wonderfully made. Knowing that there is something that makes me uniquely me. So, even if someone is doing the same thing that I'm doing, there's a way that I do it that's uniquely mine. And I pull that from hip-hop. I apply that to how I may design a workshop. I use that to encourage myself at times when I don't necessarily wake up feeling like I'm on top of my game or that I should still even be in the game.

Ian Levy, Assistant Professor of School Counseling at Manhattan College, noted the sense of acceptance he felt as a college student first trying his hand at hip-hop sealed the deal for him. He had found his cultural home. The love, welcome, and embrace he felt within the hip-hop cypher communities gave him the confidence and belonging educational institutions did not. Participating in hip-hop experiences helped Ian to overcome educational self-doubt, which is incredibly important because of the position he now holds. Many young people would never think a college professor would have had a rough time in high school. With "imposter syndrome" being such a pervasive and common experience in education for so many BIPOC students and educators (Tucker), confidence is a critically important mindset. And unapologetically displaying confidence (boasting, bragging, or talking noise) is a necessary act of resistance.

Claiming Space: Claiming space concerns entering, moving through, and transforming a space while exercising confidence in one's talent, skills, and ability. To claim space is to *own* the space. Toni Blackman, founder and executive director of Rhyme Like a Girl (RLAG), engages young women and girls in cultivating their craft as emcees from songwriting to relationship building to harnessing the power of their energy both on and off-stage. One of the many nuggets of wisdom Toni offers to the Hip-Hop Mindset conversation is the value for commanding attention and claiming space. She relates how the best emcee doesn't simply *instruct* the audience to move, rather they use their voice and their presence to *inspire* movement:

The audience will follow the rhythm and power of your voice—they will come closer to the stage, they will complete your verse, their bodies will sway in whatever direction you are swaying. You don't have to force it; they move because they feel your energy. They sense your spirit. They respect your power.

Claiming space is about harnessing power. Who is teaching future or current BIPOC teachers the skill of harnessing the power of their own voice and energy? For BIPOC communities to harness their cultural power and to "own" space in an institution, there must be a different understanding of ownership. Ownership has nothing to do with real estate deeds or even leadership positions. It is not about who bought the building or who was appointed to run it. Andre Perry's memory of witnessing one of his first hip-hop concerts provides a perfect example:

> When I saw Run DMC perform during the Fresh Fest Tour in the eighties. And he goes through that whole intro, "There's been a whole lot of people on this stage here tonight, but I want you to know one thing: This is MY house!" And when you think about that it's like wow, he was claiming space. He was claiming space in front of thousands of people. And honestly, I try to claim space too, in the same way. I approach my work with the mindset that there's been a whole lot of people before me and there might be people after me, but today this is MY house. I'm going to set the stage.

Run DMC did not own the stadium, and they were not the only artists performing that night. But yet, they claimed the arena as "their" house. They walked on stage with the intent to give the best performance ever given in that space. Moving beyond hip-hop and into sports, often sports fans may not remember the name of an arena, but they do remember historic games that were played there. They do remember the player's name who gave the mind-blowing athletic performance. Adopting a cultural mindset that allows one to walk into work or school ready and willing to academically show out transforms culturally intimidating spaces.

Commanding Attention: Commanding attention is a nod to the performative aspect of most hip-hop production. Whether it is music, canvas art, spoken word, dance, or educational instruction, hip-hop culture demands an engaging approach to the work. Commanding attention is about having a dynamic and engaging presence and knowing how to move the community. Ian Levy directly names public speaking as a skill he has gotten from hip-hop, "Being able to grab the mic and speak in the moment, not having to memorize things or use notes is a skill that I have gotten from hip-hop. I'm able to trust that I can form and connect thoughts that flow together. I'm comfortable." He goes on to discuss the ways hip-hop culture also gave him the permission to publicly express his full range of emotions in his work:

> Being able to emote in front of people is another thing I get from hip-hop. Academia is really good at making you believe that you don't need to be emotional and that you should be very scientific and objective. Hip-hop preaches the opposite. Hip-hop preaches we want to hear what you have to say, what you've been through, your pain and your happiness, everything. The range of your emotional experiences is demanded in hip-hop. And I've learned how to bring those emotional experiences to the stage. I say stage

but it might really be teaching class or giving a conference presentation. But I treat it like a performance, I really do. My mentor, Chris Emdin refers to it as being a "spitter." What he is talking about is the way that you are able to get on the mic and speak in a really engaging way—to command attention. I think that's necessary. That framing has been powerful for me because I bring that emcee energy into any space.

How does commanding attention connect to fields like education? There are many fields that require its professionals to perform on a daily basis; teaching is one of those professions. Educators at any level must possess the ability to hold the attention of an audience. Those who have the ability to move the crowd (through their speaking or actions), often excel. Those who take the performativity of teaching as serious as let's say Beyonce takes performing (innovative choreography, constant practice, dress rehearsals, mic checks) are probably able to capture students' attention because they pay so much attention to their craft. Understanding the power of voice and showing up in one's profession is critical. Andre Perry also firmly identified hip-hop as his source for developing his skills as a public scholar and educator:

> The other thing [I get from hip-hop] is my movement in the world. I'm talking about my physical movements here. When I'm giving a presentation, I know how to get the crowd going and get the crowd hyped. I get that from hip-hop. I observed in hip-hop how emcees control the mic, how they control a stage, how they keep a crowd's attention. So, you can't have great content (important data) with a flow that is whack. No one will listen. You will lose people.

These are critical skillsets for any educator; however, these skills are not always a point of focus in educational training. Educators who want to engage Black and Brown students can start by not boring them. African Diasporic people come from a long cultural tradition that values strong oratory, vibrant expression, and lively movement. In other words, some cultures are inherently hype. Michael Benitez offers a wonderful summary of how commanding attention is so powerful as a cultural mindset. In his role as a university Vice President, the pressure to perform "professionalism" in very particular, white culturally normed ways is very real and very present in his career; but he relies on hip-hop culture to guide his professional approach:

> I'd say the last skill I learned from hip-hop is stage presence or showmanship. You've got to see me in leadership team meetings. It's really an interesting place because everybody's learning. My colleagues are learning new ideas about what professionalism could like. They are learning new language and expressions. They are learning to relax and be free. Hip-hop influences how I do institution-wide listening sessions on my campus, how I teach, how I facilitate workshops. When you engage through a hip-hop lens, you truly draw participants and the audience in like drawing in a concert crowd—active engagement as part of the community. So, I'm always engaging a back and forth with the community-call and response. The campus community also knows, in those moments, that I'm truly listening and that I'm including

their voices. Honestly, it's not just including their voices, but it's also the acknowledgement of their feelings and how they are present in that space. The emcee needs the audience as much as the audience needs the emcee. It's like I am asking them, "Are you with me?" or better yet, "Holler if you hear me." I want them to get loud, not quiet in their response and feedback.

The bottom line is education must be enlivened in some way so that educators and students can be more energized by it.

Conclusion

This project has prompted me to consider what might happen if Hip-Hop Mindset practices were more broadly adopted by educators as a professional approach. I do not mean educators simply working to develop or support these practices among students by including hip-hop culture in educational settings. The inclusion of hip-hop culture needs to happen, but a Hip-Hop Mindset is about more than the inclusion of hip hop culture. Hip-Hop Mindset practices can inform how educators show up in their professional lives and allow space for them to grow and develop not only *what they do* in their schools or on their campuses, but also *who they are* in their schools or on their campuses. The cultural literacy the Hip-Hop Mindset provides about the nature of hip-hop—the ideologies, values, beliefs, practices, habits, and proclivities present among community members—helps educators (who have been urged to adopt hip-hop pedagogical approaches) to see and understand hip-hop as a culture more deeply. Hip-hop creates more than music and rhymes, it develops "ways of being" rooted in ethics of excellence. This work also affirms those professionals and educators who already show up hip-hop in all they do.

Situating hip-hop as a professional mindset and a critical form of professional development acknowledges historically-BIPOC cultural ways of knowing and being as viable success strategies. Hip-hop culture can historically be considered a BIPOC cultural form because it was created by BIPOC youth. While many BIPOC educators and students do not identify with hip-hop culture, there are many others who do. Love (*Hip Hop's Li'l Sistas Speak*), shares why a value for and embrace of hip-hop culture is necessary for the current generation of educators:

> Our teaching force currently, and over the next ten to twenty years, is young and influenced by Hip Hop, no matter the teachers' race, gender, class or sexuality. Many Black and Brown students who enter into teaching will embody Hip Hop. Therefore, we need school officials to allow teachers to bring themselves and their culture into the classroom, so teachers and students feel culturally affirmed in their learning environments. (112)

Love describes the natural and organic approach already being used by many educators as an important social justice possibility that has yet to be broadly acknowledged or tapped within the larger educational institution. A Hip-Hop Mindset is not a cultural costume an educator can "put on." It is a way of thinking or mode of being that requires looking inward to engage the process of becoming more authentic through one's work. I share my personal stories in my interpretation of the research because we are all in this together. In the article, "We've Been Doing It Your Way Long Enough," the authors champion the idea of education being a syncretic process in which "human beings work together, drawing on multiple resources to co-construct and reinvent practices. These constructions are inherently complex and embody the contradictions and potential for learning by emphasizing the cultural richness of home and community practices typically characterized as deficient" (Baines et. al., 420).

They further expand this idea by suggesting that in our contemporary world, which is tied to so many years of educational oppression, educators cannot simply dive into doing something new. Rather they must engage in a critical form of practice that pushes them to not only add new perspectives, voices, and resources but also critically evaluate current resources, practices and structures for power differentials, contemporary ideologies of patriarchy, racism, anti-blackness, white supremacy, and cultural deficiency. In other words, educators cannot simply add a new practice—they must critically interrogate the whole of their practice. A critical part of interrogating the whole, must include the cultural mindsets educators bring to their work. Educators must move beyond identifying biases or internalized racist beliefs within their own cultural worldviews and shift their ideas about professional and academic ways of being.

The outcomes of this project, situate a Hip-Hop Mindset as more than a success mindset, but rather a mindset of cultural efficacy and cultural freedom. It posits hip-hop culture as a producer of important knowledge, skills, values and practices that can build important forms of cultural literacy (through its demand for cultural integrity and authenticity) and critical literacy (through its demand for truth telling and social critique). The Hip-Hop Mindset gives students and educators the permission to show up in life as their full, authentic cultural selves. This permission is a powerful act of social justice in an education system that has been trying to change BIPOC students and educators from its inception.

Works Cited

Adjapong, Edmund S., and Christopher Emdin. "Rethinking Pedagogy in Urban Spaces: Implementing Hip-Hop Pedagogy in The Urban Science Classroom." *Journal of Urban Learning, Teaching and Research*, vol. 11, 2015, pp. 66-77.

Asante, Molefi Kete. *Revolutionary Pedagogy*. Universal Write Publications LLC, 2017.

Baines, Janice, et al. *"We've Been Doing It Your Way Long Enough": Choosing the Culturally Relevant Classroom (Language and Literacy Series)*. Teachers College Press, 2018.

Boutte, Gloria Swindler. *Educating African American Students: And How Are the Children?* Routledge, 2015.

Boutte, Gloria, et al. "Using African Diaspora Literacy to Heal and Restore the Souls of Young Black Children." *International Critical Childhood Policy Studies*, vol 6, no. 1, 2017, pp. 66-79.

Boyer, Ernest L. *Scholarship Reconsidered: Priorities of the Professoriate*. Princeton University Press, 1997.

Bradley, Regina. *Boondock Kollage: Stories from the Hip Hop South*. Peter Lang Publishing Inc., 2017.

Brown, Ruth Nicole. *Hear Our Truths: The Creative Potential of Black Girlhood*. University of Illinois Press, Champagne, Ill, 2013.

Bump, Bethany. "Can You Be 'Ratchet' and Academic? This Professor Thinks So." *Times Union*, 7 Nov 2017, www.timesunion.com/news/article/Can-you-be-ratchet-and-academic-This-professor-12339078.php

Caven, Meghan. "Why We Need an Anti-Racist Approach to Social and Emotional Learning." *EDC*, 27 July, 2020, www.edc.org/blog/why-we-need-anti-racist-approach-social-and-emotional-learning.

Chang, Jeff, and Kool Herc. *Can't Stop Won't Stop: A History of the Hip-Hop Generation*. Picador, 2005.

Dimitriadis, Greg. *Performing Identity/Performing Culture: Hip Hop as Text, Pedagogy and Lived Practice*. Peter Lang, 2001.

Emdin, Christopher. *For White Folks Who Teach in the Hood... and the Rest of Y'all Too: Reality Pedagogy and Urban Education (Race, Education, and Democracy)*. Reprint ed., Beacon Press, 2017.

Endsley, Crystal Leigh. *The Fifth Element: Social Justice Pedagogy through Spoken Word Poetry*. Sunny Press, 2017.

Gonzalez, Norma, et al. *Funds of Knowledge: Theorizing Practices in Households, Communities, and Classrooms*. Routledge, 2005.

Hill, Marc Lamont, and Emery Petchauer, editors. *Schooling Hip-Hop: Expanding Hip-Hop Based Education across the Curriculum*. Illustrated ed., Teachers College Press, 2013.

Jenkins, Toby S. "A Beautiful Mind: Black Male Intellectual Identity in Hip-Hop Culture." *Journal of Black Studies*, vol. 42, no. 8, 2011, pp. 1231-1251. doi:10.1177/0021934711405050.

—. *My Culture, My Color, My Self: Heritage, Resilience, and Community in the Lives of Young Adults*. Temple University Press, 2013.

Jenkins, Toby S., et al., editors. *Open Mic Night: Campus Programs that Champion College Student Voice and Engagement*. Stylus Publishing, 2017.

Jupp, Victor, editor. *The SAGE Dictionary of Social Research Methods*. SAGE Publications Ltd, 2006. doi:10.4135/9780857020116.

Kelly, Lauren L. "Listening Differently: Youth Self-Actualization through Critical Hip Hop Literacies." *English Teaching: Practice & Critique*, vol. 19, no. 3, 2020, pp. 269-285. doi:10.1108/ETPC-08-2019-0106.

—. "'I am not Jasmine; I am Aladdin': How Youth Challenge Structural Inequity through Critical Hip Hop Literacies." *International Journal of Critical Media Literacy*, vol. 1, no. 2, 2020, pp. 9-30. doi:10.1163/25900110-00201002.

Kerka, Sandra. "Community Asset Mapping" U.S. Needs Assessment, Educational Resource Information Center, No. 47, 2003

King, Joyce E, editor. *Black Education: A Transformative Research and Action Agenda for the New Century*. Routledge, 2005.

McKnight, J.L. & Kretsmann, J.P. "Mapping Community Capacity" in Minkler, M. (1997) *Community Organizing and Community Building for Health*, Rutgers University Press, New Brunswick, NJ.

KRS-One. *The Gospel of Hip Hop: First Instrument*. powerHouse Books, 2009.

Lawrence-Lightfoot, Sara, and Jessica Hoffmann Davis. *The Art and Science of Portraiture*. Jossey-Bass, 1997.

Love, Bettina L. *Hip Hop's Li'l Sistas Speak: Negotiating Hip Hop Identities and Politics in the New South*. Peter Lang, 2012.

—. "Complex Personhood of Hip Hop & the Sensibilities of the Culture that Fosters Knowledge of Self & Self-Determination." *Equity & Excellence in Education*, vol. 49, no. 4, 2016, pp. 414–427. doi:10.1080/10665684.2016.1227223.

—. "Anti-Black State Violence, Classroom Edition: The Spirit Murdering of Black Children." *Journal of Curriculum and Pedagogy*, vol. 13, no. 1, 2016, pp. 22–25. Crossref, doi:10.1080/15505170.2016.1138258.

Marable, Manning. *Black Leadership*. Columbia University Press, 1998

Merriam-Webster. *Merriam-Webster's Dictionary and Thesaurus*. Revised and updated ed., Merriam-Webster, 2020.

Morrell, Ernest. (2002). "Toward a Critical Pedagogy of Popular Culture: Literacy Development among Urban Youth." *Journal of Adolescent & Adult Literacy*, vol. 46, no. 1, pp. 72-77. JSTOR, www.jstor.org/stable/40017507.

Oluo, Ijeoma. *So You Want to Talk about Race*. Seal Press, 2019.

Perry, Andre M. *Know Your Price: Valuing Black Lives and Property in America's Black Cities*. Brookings Institution Press, 2020. JSTOR, www.jstor.org/stable/10.7864/j.ctvbd8mdd.

Petchauer, Emery. "Framing and Reviewing Hip-Hop Educational Research." *Review of Educational Research*, Vol. 79, No. 2, June 2009, pp. 946–978.

Rautins, Cara, and Awad Ibrahim. "Wide-Awakeness: Toward a critical pedagogy of imagination, humanism, agency, and becoming." *The International Journal of Critical Pedagogy*, vol. 3, no. 3, 2011, pp 24-36.

Richardson, Elaine. *Hiphop Literacies*. Routledge, 2006.

Rose, Tricia. *Black Noise: Rap Music and Black Culture in Contemporary America*. Illustrated ed., Wesleyan University Press, 1994.

Runell, Marcella, and Martha Diaz. *The Hip-Hop Education Guidebook Volume 1*. Hip-Hop Association, 2007.

Stovall, David. "We can Relate: Hip-Hop Culture, Critical Pedagogy, and the Secondary Classroom." *Urban Education*, vol. 41, no. 6, 2006, pp. 585-602. doi:10.1177/0042085906292513.

Tucker, Melanie V. "Rewriting the Narrative on Imposter Syndrome." *Women in Higher Education*, vol. 30, no. 4, 2021, pp. 1-2.

Yosso, Tara. "Whose Culture Has Capital? A Critical Race Theory Discussion of Community Cultural Wealth." *Race and Ethnicity in Education*, vol. 8, no. 1, 2005, pp. 69-91. doi: 10.1080/1361332052000341006

Author Bio

Dr. Toby S. Jenkins is an Associate Professor of Higher Education Administration and Interim Associate Dean of Diversity, Equity & Inclusion in the Graduate School at the University of South Carolina. At UofSC, she also serves as Director of the Museum of Education, a research center located in the College of Education. Her scholarship focuses on cultural inclusion in higher education. She is particularly concerned with the ways culture serves as a politic of social survival, a tool of social change, and a critical space of institutional transformation. Jenki279@mailbox.sc.edu

"An Art of Truth in Things": Confronting Hiphop Illiteracies in Writing Classrooms at Predominantly White Colleges and Universities

Tessa Brown

Abstract

This article interrogates how hiphop composition pedagogies can interrupt what the author terms the "hiphop illiteracies" that circulate in predominantly white institutions (PWIs). An analysis of four college writing classrooms that integrate hiphop texts at one PWI reveals pervasive anti-Blackness in student attitudes, but also in the research and course design as well as in department-mandated course texts. The analysis demonstrates the need for writing pedagogies that name and teach Black language, writing, and meaning-making practices while also asking students, teachers, and administrators to reflexively examine their own identities' locations vis-a-vis those practices. The author advocates a reflexive pedagogy that asks students to locate themselves vis-a-vis power as a starting point for investigations of language and culture. The author concludes that hiphop pedagogies have significant critical social justice possibilities in institutionally white educational contexts, but these benefits are not automatic and demand pedagogies of reflexivity, sociolinguistics, and intersectional feminism.

Keywords

AAVE, anti-Blackness, hiphop pedagogy, PWIs, reflexivity, whiteness, writing studies

In an Instagram post from Spring 2014, rapper 2 Chainz is photographed from behind, facing an arena full of fans, his arms outstretched above him, his locs hanging down his back. The audience, washed out by the lights backlighting the star, fills the floor and three balconies of a college sports arena. Their arms raised in ecstasy, the rapper's fans appear overwhelmingly white. Beneath the posted photo is 2 Chainz's caption: "[Central New York] University was a Movie." While the growing literature on hiphop pedagogies overwhelmingly focuses on educating students of color using hiphop styles and texts in classrooms (e.g., R. Brown, Craig and Kynard, Green, Hill, Kirkland, Lindsey, Love), 2 Chainz's concert at what I call Central New York University (CNYU), held while I was conducting my research on hiphop pedagogy there, points to the need to engage with white students' and white educational institutions' participation in hiphop culture and pedagogy. As of 2017, hiphop was the most popular music genre in America (Sanfiorenzo). A quick walk around campus housing on a Friday or Saturday night at a Predominantly White Institution (PWI)—or a scroll through Tiktok's most popular white influencers' feeds—can quickly demonstrate the massive consumption of hiphop sounds, fashion, gesture and language by white and other non-Black American youth.

These hiphop expressions are a subset of what Elaine Richardson terms "African American Vernacular Discourse" (1), the unique communication practices shared by Black Americans. This discourse includes, but is not limited to, the linguistics of African American Vernacular English, a distinct, grammatical variety of English that has unique phonetics (sounds and pronunciation), lexicon (words), and grammar that descend from West African languages. AAVE's sounds and meanings are shaped by continued segregation, oppression, and joy of African-descended peoples in the United States, even as Black communities continue to negotiate ambivalence around the power and appropriateness of the language in a range of settings (Jordan, Richardson, Smitherman). Yet Richardson also acknowledges that hiphop artists are not producing discourse exclusively within and for Black communities. Rather, hiphop artists are "performing products" (12) whose personas are created in negotiation with the demands and desires of white audiences and white-led entertainment companies. These mass-marketed representations of Black people can cater to white imaginations of Black folks as hypersexual, violent, or criminal (Hurt, Love, Lindsey). At CNYU, 2 Chainz's visit also coincided with an explosion of racist discourses on campus, including the circulation of a video of a white student-athlete using the n-word, which some attributed to her proximity to Black friends and Black musics ("Hanna Strong"). These contradictory occurrences reflect the paradoxical nature of anti-Blackness, as racist tropes and behaviors about and toward Black people circulate *alongside and in tandem with* the enthusiastic consumption of Black cultural products. While this event and others provoked anti-racist activism on the CNYU campus (Samuels, Democratizing Knowledge Collective), they are also an ongoing occasion for teacher-scholars to interrogate the possibilities and risks of hiphop pedagogies in predominantly white spaces.

Following Richardson's eponymous study of Black artists' production of "hiphop literacies," in this study, conducted in four college writing classrooms at one PWI, I inquire about hiphop *il*-literacies and ask how hiphop writing pedagogies can promote critical engagement with mass-produced hiphop and language and literacy in majority-white classrooms. My findings show that while hiphop easily engages students, classrooms will reproduce existing hiphop illiteracies without careful course material on Black Language, linguistic racism, and intersectional feminism. Hiphop pedagogies' social justice possibilities and risks are shaped by the paradoxes of hiphop fandom more broadly. In the United States, hiphop's uptake by white fans is complex and contradictory, as white hiphoppers' identification with rap's resistive politics is shaped by decreasing opportunities for all Americans (Kitwana, hooks qtd. in Kirkland) even as consumption can veer into the fetishistic and anti-Black (Yousman). In this context, the growing numbers of programs and institutes in predominantly-white higher education institutions like Harvard, Stanford, Cornell, Tulane, Duke, the University of Virginia and the University of Arizona themselves must be interrogated, even as these programs create space for scholars and students to engage hiphop studies' interdisciplinary attention to language, literacy, and education; sound production and digital technologies; the arts and performance; studies of space and place; and more. The entrenched and growing presence of hiphop education in predominantly and historically white spaces demands attention to how hiphop circulates in these school and campus communities and how it is engaged in classrooms at PWIs that may or may not themselves be predominantly white.

My own identity as a white Jewish woman hiphop pedagogue who has been teaching at PWIs for ten years also keys me into the need to interrogate hiphop instruction in these contexts led by white instructors. Studies on the accelerating appropriation of Black discourses by white youth via social media have continually pointed to anti-Blackness as the frame that makes sense of the unceasing commodification of Black people, Black culture, and even Black affect in United States history (Judy, Parham, Sobande). Understanding anti-Blackness means seeing commodification of Black culture and Black people as central to American capitalism. Beyond the exploitation of Black labor that is perpetuated through racialized systems of poverty and incarceration, anti-Blackness is critical cultural theory that plots the throughline from the original commodification of enslaved Africans, to the fundamentality of exploited Black artists and sounds to American musical history, to contemporary non-Black youths' accelerating uptake of Black cultural practices and forms including language, fashion and makeup, and physicality and dance (see Lorenz).

As theorists of Black language and literacy pedagogy increasingly insist language educators celebrate Black students'—and all nonstandard-English-speaking students'—use of their home discourses in literacy classrooms (Baker-Bell, Young et al), hiphop emerges as a site for helping students recognize and appreciate Black cultural practices. This work needs to be approached carefully by and for those outside Black communities, as Black scholars have demonstrated that despite widespread AAVE usage among Black Americans, community members themselves can use or even celebrate Black discourse practices while disagreeing on the circumstances of its deployment (Jordan, Smitherman). This study builds on others which insist we help students engage hiphop critically, appreciating artists' genius but also interrogating how mass-mediated hiphop songs and images cater to dominant stereotypes about Black language and Black people, including in specifically gendered ways that pigeonhole youth of color into exaggerated gender roles (Lindsey, Love). As hiphop pedagogues, we must explicitly and dialectically engage hiphop's contradictory cultural behavior as both a resistive Black art form and as a site of appropriation and misrepresentation by non-Black people. We must also engage an intersectional feminist lens that draws attention specifically to Black women's and Black LGBTQIA people's experiences in hiphop, and how hiphop's gendered messages shape widespread perceptions of Black gendered identities (Lindsey). Engaging Black art, white consumption, and anti-Blackness demands educators push through what Eduardo Bonilla-Silva terms "colorblind racism," a denial of race that protects racial inequalities by refusing race itself—as a reality, and as a category of analysis that can promote anti-racist remedies.

In his analysis of interviews about race with white people and people of color, Bonilla-Silva demonstrates how colorblindness as a rhetorical strategy for racism manifests in contemporary whites' near-inability to discuss racial realities in clear terms, a phenomenon reflected upon by the students in this study. Because "whiteness refers to a set of cultural practices that are usually unmarked and unnamed" (Frankenburg qtd. in Hunter and Nettles 388), examining racialized discourses involves not only what is said but what is unsaid, what is included as well as what is omitted. Taking a stance against colorblindness and whiteness means not just acknowledging difference but actively assuming an "antiracist," versus a nonracist, stance (Bonilla-Silva 15-16). Refusing to name race protects what Bonilla-Silva terms the "white habitus," a way of being that "creates and conditions [white people's] views, cognitions, and even sense of beauty" (123). Arguing that "race and whiteness structure our thinking" (10) and, ultimately, our research design, Kirsch and Ritchie promote a "rigorously reflexive examination of ourselves as researchers that is as careful as our observation of the objects of our inquiry" (9). My study contributes to our understanding of linguistic ideologies within the white habitus at one PWI, and the mis-understandings white and non-white students hold about language, fluency, and intelligence that can fester when reflexivity is not practiced, which I term hiphop illiteracies.

Within English education, hiphop pedagogies include education in both literature and literary analysis as well as critical language pedagogies that center on hiphop's prominent use of Black discourse practices, particularly African American Vernacular English (AAVE), educating students to the variety of linguistic discourses and the ways in which power governs socially privileged and marginalized language practices (Alim). Hiphop composition studies can be situated within a wider terrain of hiphop language, literacy, and literary studies. Studies of hiphop in K-12 language arts classrooms with student of color populations show that positioning hiphop lyrics as literary texts develops students' literary analysis skills, and can open up conversations on identity, violence, trauma, gender, and representation that support students' self-esteem and engagement (Hill, Love, R. Brown). Hiphop's multimodal culture of "5 elements"—rapping, producing, breakdancing, graffiti, and dropping knowledge—has been an object of literary and rhetorical study since at least Tricia Rose's fundamental 1994 *Black Noise*, which attended to both the rebellious, griot-descended verses of rap lyrics as well as the Afrodiasporic loops and ruptures of analog and digital hiphop beats. Within composition studies, which focuses on writing education for college-aged students, hiphop scholars are at the forefront of theorizing how 21st-century writers and mixed-media composers use digital technologies to make meaning in fragmented, hypercirculatory media environments and how these hyper-contemporary practices can help educators craft more relevant pedagogies for students (Banks, Craig and Kynard, Green). My own survey of colleagues teaching hiphop in college composition classrooms found that college writing instructors use hiphop texts as objects of analysis for traditional academic writing, and also invite students to produce hiphop genres like mixtapes and liner notes (T. Brown "Schooled"), a practice also discussed by hiphop educators like Banks.

Methods and Findings: Emergent Anti-Blackness in the Classroom

In order to understand the benefits, risks, and impacts of a hiphop composition pedagogy at a PWI, I conducted a classroom study of four such courses, two taught by myself, and two more taught by a colleague, the Black American writer Nana Adjei-Brenyah, a fellow graduate student at the time and now a successful published author. As I discuss extensively below, this study demonstrated the need for composition courses in predominantly white contexts to confront and illuminate anti-Blackness, including linguistic anti-Blackness. Through the grounded analysis of ethnographic notes, student exit interviews, my own teaching, and department-mandated curricular materials, I located anti-Blackness not just in student attitudes but in my own research design as well as in the textbook I used (see Brown "What Else" for a fuller discussion). Research shows that writing students learn best when their complete identities, including but not limited to their linguistic identities, are welcomed into the room (Ball and Ellis, Ivanić). Yet by attempting to teach a hiphop composition pedagogy without creating opportunities for students to reflect on their own inextricably raced and gendered identities, my course, and to a lesser extent, my colleague's, preserved a colorblind environment in the classroom that limited students' understandings of the power dynamics of language prestige and language subordination and their own participation in these systems. And all of our courses failed to teach about AAVE as a condition for understanding hiphop discourses, thus perpetuating our students' hiphop illiteracies.

Ultimately, my analysis demonstrates the need for writing pedagogies that name and teach Black language, writing, and meaning-making practices while also asking students, teachers, and administrators to reflexively examine their own identities' locations vis-a-vis those practices. While hiphop pedagogies have significant critical social justice possibilities at PWIs, they also come with risks that must be addressed head-on through practices and pedagogies that center Black discourses, reflexivity, and intersectional feminism. In the context of the predominantly white university, hiphop becomes a vehicle for all composition students to understand how Blackness and anti-Blackness circulate through our everyday language, challenging students to move towards more explicit and reflexive relationships to their language choices. My research suggests that teaching and practicing reflexivity are core solutions to the paradoxical rhetorical action of hiphop in predominantly white spaces. I advocate a reflexive pedagogy of power and identity that asks students to locate themselves vis-a-vis power as a starting point for investigations of language and culture. As I show in this study, hiphop pedagogies have significant critical social justice possibilities in institutionally white educational contexts, but these benefits are not automatic and demand pedagogies of reflexivity, sociolinguistics, and intersectional feminism.

There were four classes in the study: a freshman required writing course taught by me; a sophomore required writing course taught by me, and two sections of a sophomore required writing class taught by Nana, then a master's student in creative writing. I was a doctoral student during the study, and Nana and I designed our own curricula in accordance with broad dictates from our program, while also integrating hiphop materials in consultation with one another. This IRB-approved study allowed me to collect ethnographic notes during and after classes, and collect student writings (n=60) and conduct interviews (n=20) with participating students. Students in all four classes wrote drafts and revisions of 3 papers, including literacy narratives, close readings, and research papers. All were taught during the 2013–2014 school year at Central New York University, a private Research-1 university in upstate (locals would say Central) New York. The surrounding city itself has a large Black population ringed by predominantly white suburbs and was shaped by late 20th century segregationist practices like white flight, systemic Black poverty, unaccountable city services, and violent policing.

The students in this study were exposed to three separate, but similar, curricula. My freshmen and sophomore courses integrated hiphop songs, videos, and scholarship that engaged themes of literacy, discourse, the writing process, citation use, and Black Language with non-hiphop texts from writing studies on the same themes. Nana's two sections of his sophomore course focused on hiphop culture as a subject of inquiry. Although he did not incorporate many texts from writing studies, literacy, or composition research, he presented rappers as writers making purposeful writerly and rhetorical choices, and challenged students to see rappers' lyrics, musical choices, and visuals as purposive, meaningful, and contextually responsive. All three classes opened with and were framed by Tony Silver's graffiti documentary *Style Wars*, which explicitly engages questions of writing, multimodality, rhetorical effectiveness, and the writing process, as well as with either the entire album or tracks from Kanye West's debut album *The College Dropout*, which both implicitly demonstrates and explicitly engages with questions of rhetorically appropriate discourse choices and African-American compositional style. All students also read Joseph Harris's chapter "Coming to Terms," from his book *Rewriting*. Students in my classes engaged with writing studies scholarship by authors like Deborah Brandt, James Paul Gee, John Swales, and Rebecca Moore Howard, as well as writing studies scholarship that more closely addressed hiphop and Black language and rhetorical practices by authors like Tricia Rose, H. Samy Alim, Geneva Smitherman, and David Kirkland. Nana's sophomore students also engaged with dialect diversity through June Jordan's essay "Nobody Mean More to Me Than You and the Future Life of Willie Jordan."

While I read and reviewed student writings and my ethnographic notes, I limited my qualitative coding practice to transcripts of the 20 student interviews I conducted. Instead of working to assess my students' writing and "grade" them in my analysis to determine what or how much students learned, I instead let students tell me for themselves what they learned, how they evolved as writers and critical thinkers, and how they felt about the course they had just taken. All participating students received strong final grades of As or Bs in the courses, and as you will see in the discussion, I was still able to assess student learning through their oral reporting of processes and concepts they encountered. This focus on interviews corresponds with the feminist methodological principle of co-creation of knowledge with research participants, and echoes the assessment priorities expressed by Toni Cade Bambara, unearthed in my archival research elsewhere, that students can orally self-assess when given "uninterrupted time to rap" (qtd. in T. Brown "Let the People Rap" 120). Since students who came in for interviews overwhelmingly (though not exclusively) enjoyed the course and touted their own learning about writing, these data ultimately illustrate how and why hiphop worked in the composition classroom for students who did respond positively to the material. The interviews illustrate broader attitudes about race, language, and culture that extend beyond measuring learning outcomes, but they also show that students' mastery of general topics in writing far outpaced their understandings of sociolinguistic concepts.

Following a grounded theory methodology (Charmaz), I open-coded and wrote coding memos throughout the data analysis process as I developed my theory. By repeatedly coding these 20 transcripts in order to consolidate and clarify my codes (Saldaña), I ended up with 8 main codes, which I further consolidated into 3 major phenomena (See Table 1, below). During my open coding stages, I noted identity, affect, genre, and transfer as preliminary themes. Eventually, the coding process uncovered the trenchant anti-Blackness in my students' relationships to hiphop, standard English, and Black Language, an anti-Blackness that existed among students of all races and genders, both longtime hiphop fans and those new to the genre. It also showed the white habitus of the classroom and even my research design, as I noticed a totalizing binary between whiteness and Blackness, with almost nonexistent opportunities for Asian, Latinx, or Indigenous students to self-identify or be culturally recognized. The coding process also revealed to me students' deep identifications with hiphop pedagogy. I found that hiphop, a contradictory art form which is both resistive and commodified, *rhetorically appeals to students learning in the contradictory ideological context of anti-Black commodity capitalism*. As such, I conclude that teachers must make personal decisions, rendered public to students, about whether hiphop will be mobilized merely to engage students in the acts of writing and research for individualistic gain or whether hiphop will be critiqued towards solidarity-building understandings of literacy, writing, and discourse which are consistent with the knowledge of our field.

In my preliminary analysis of interview transcripts, I realized that I had not requested students' self-identifications by race, gender, or other demographic markers. Recognizing this, I added a question in the interviews I had not conducted yet; thus, some students gave fuller accounts of their own identities and how those identities shaped their experiences of the course. In the discussion of student interviews that follows, I identify students by race or other signifiers only when they did so themselves. Recognizing my own failure to invite students to self-identify further shaped my recognition of the way I had perpetuated the white habitus in class and shaped the analysis itself, below. According to student preferences, some student names are pseudonyms and others are not. I proceed with referring to Nana as my colleague to keep the focus on our students. When editing student interview excerpts for publication, I removed some fillers (um, like, you know) but retained others to preserve the flavor of the language. I preserve students' natural language and do not use [sic] markings.

Table 1: Codes, Frequencies, and Phenomena

	My students	Colleague's students	Totals	Combined phenomena
1. Identification grounds investment *Students remark that their investment in or engagement with course materials and assignments was facilitated by the relevance of course materials to their own experiences and interests*	12/13	7/7	19/20	Affective identification grounds all students' investment in the writing and research process and promotes overall criticality and investment in learning
2. Metacognitive understanding of writing as a process *Students describe their own writing process, recognize it as evolving in the class, and/or recognize writing as a process all writers go through*	13/13	7/7	20/20	
3. Reading or listening more deeply *Students say the class has led them to interrogate texts more deeply, whether reading more deeply into written texts or listening more carefully to hiphop or other music*	4/13	5/7	9/20	
4. Literacy as an evolving, situated practice *Students display an understanding of literacy as a broad array of reading and writing practices that occur in situated contexts and evolve over time*	4/13	5/7	9/20	My writing studies and my colleague's creative writing approaches to composition using hiphop both helped some of our students appreciate the rhetoricity and value of all texts, but in different ways
5. Texts, genres, and discourses as rhetorically situated *Students recognize all texts, genres, and discourses as responding to rhetorical situations that involve audiences, goals, physical contexts, timing, community norms, and other rhetorical parameters*	10/13	3/7	13/20	

	My students	Colleague's students	Totals	Combined phenomena
6. Social construction of error *Students acknowledge that error is a political rather than a linguistic reality and that error and correctness are not static but are rather rooted in rhetorical situations*	9/13	0/7	9/20	Despite hiphop fandom, anti-Blackness is widespread in student understandings of language and culture and whiteness was the default classroom habitus in all classes studied, as reflected in about half of student interviews. [Recommendation: Thus, AAVE, white supremacy, and linguistic discrimination must be explicitly named and taught to be understood and to disrupt classroom whiteness]
7. Depictions of Anti-Blackness *Students affirm or confront stereotypes around Black people or Black musics, as well as white students' comments that they have been derided by white peers for enjoying Black musics*	8/13	6/7	14/20	
8. Encountering the white habitus in class *Students affirm white discourse norms in class including fear of discussing race or the whiteness of the classroom environment. Includes places where students of color identify racialized tensions in class as well as where white students affirm that there is no racialized tension in class*	6/13	5/7	11/20	

Despite the limitations of my research design, student exit interviews were instructive in demonstrating the critical social justice possibilities for hiphop composition pedagogy in predominantly white environments—and the stakes and challenges for educators navigating these contexts. Students' interviews are complex as they reflect pedagogical failures and successes, while richly testifying to students' learning, struggling, and thriving in the context of colorblind capitalism, anti-Black violence and the emerging Black Lives Matter liberation movement. Interview transcripts show students negotiating dominant and resistive discourses about literacy, language, and linguistic racism, and the insufficiency of sociolinguistic lessons.

I found that

- (1) Affective identification with hiphop and multimedia course material grounds all students' investment in the writing and research process and promotes overall criticality and investment in learning;
- (2) My writing studies and my colleague's creative writing approaches using hiphop both helped some of our students appreciate the rhetoricity and value of all texts, but in different ways;

- (3) Despite hiphop fandom, anti-Blackness is widespread in student understandings of language and culture, and whiteness is the default classroom habitus, as reflected in about half of student interviews.
- **Recommendation:** AAVE, white supremacy, and linguistic discrimination must be explicitly named and taught to be understood and to disrupt classroom whiteness.

The phrase I ultimately chose for my first code, **identification grounds investment**, reflects students' repeated reflections of education as a market in which one exchanges resources like time, interest, and energy for returns like grades and future financial success. This code was ubiquitous in student interviews, as was my second code, **metacognitive understanding of writing as a process.** Together, these two codes showed that students found it easier to pay attention, understand course concepts from writing and hiphop studies, and move through the research and writing because of the relevance of hiphop, its connection to current events, and their freedom to choose research projects that resonated. Further, a third prominent code, **reading or listening more deeply,** indicated that this increased investment and positive affect in class helped students develop their criticality, engage with challenging concepts, and confront the ambient anti-Blackness that had precluded them from fully *hearing* the hiphop texts they already enjoyed.

Students' understanding of literacy studies concepts developed differently based on my own and my colleague's pedagogies. My attention to literacy concepts meant that more of my students than my colleague's recognized **texts, genres, and discourses as rhetorically situated** (code 5). Surprisingly, given my colleague didn't explicitly teach using a new literacies framework (Street), both his students and mine recognized **literacy as an evolving, situated practice** (code 4), suggesting perhaps that honoring rap inherently helped students validate a wider range of texts and literacy practices. With my colleague's creative writing approach, however, his students described consciously writing to engage audiences while my students did not. My students also became aware of the anti-Black and anti-youth **social construction of error** (code 6) in popular assessments of language, whereas my colleague's students didn't evidence this knowledge at all. (The name of this code comes from Chris Anson's acknowledgement that all writers and speakers make errors, but that which errors get focused on are often shaped by cultural scripts.)

Both code 6, **social constructions of error**, and code 3, **reading or listening more deeply,** overlapped significantly with code 7, **depictions of anti-Blackness**. In discussing error and listening, students reproduced and critiqued anti-Black discourses that dismiss rappers and Black Language users as ignorant and illiterate and therefore not worth listening to. Students' comments reflecting the **social construction of error** reflected how error had been socially constructed to privilege white standard speech, leaving them thinking that Black speech and Black speakers were ungrammatical, lazy, or wrong. For many of them, class introduced them to the idea that Black language choices are purposive, meaningful, contextually appropriate, and rooted in the languages of the African diaspora. While only my students could name AAVE and linguistic racism, and often only with introductory success, my colleague's students also reported that the class helped them recognize the intentionality behind Black artists' hiphop compositions. Black, white, and Asian students all described how both my own and my colleague's courses helped them notice and combat anti-Black linguistic attitudes. Finally, in order to identify the **white habitus in class** (code 8), I had to key into lapses and evasions. This code occurred when students described what they couldn't, wouldn't, or were afraid to say about race and racism, or where they described white logics or white students dominating class conversation.

Students Voicing Hiphop Literacies and Illiteracies

We can see the interrelatedness of the codes and the phenomena in comments from Jonathan, a Black sophomore in one of my courses. A computer science major, Jonathan relied heavily on the language of investment in explaining the effort he gave the course:

> ... basically if you wanna invest my time into actually doing this project, cause I'm not giving in like two hours after I've started writing—so it's like, this is not so bad, I'm reading all these stories that either a) I've read before or b) I actually enjoy reading about the person, so I'm going to keep reading, keep researching, taking this information and producing something worth the professor reading basically.

Jonathan contrasted this investment with a feeling he usually encountered in his writing process of "giving in." Jonathan felt that instructors "should like, pay attention more to tailoring our prereq[isite]s to be meaningful to what we actually wanna—basically, make it something that we would want to invest our time in." Jonathan even went so far as to suggest that this engagement in and identification with the course protected him against committing plagiarism. This comment was deeply affective, as Jonathan charted the spectrum between "the fear of plagiarizing" when writing about "old texts" and the "refreshing" sense of creating new knowledge:

> This whole like fear of plagiarizing is very hard when we're like recycling these old texts, and it's like, there's only so much that can be said about this text that has been around like forty years. I'm pretty sure the majority of things that can be studied of them, have been said, so it's like what more can I say when I'm researching all these things....So since hiphop is relatively new, the time frame is thirty years, there's not that much done on it yet, and we were bringing out even more relevant topics that happened in the last ten years, so like, that was a very refreshing thing, like, oh I can let out all my thoughts and it not be mistaken for someone else's...it's either that or like, what more can I do with this text that I don't even, I don't even relate to, I don't even, basically care about, like tomorrow I'm not even going to be thinking about this topic after I turn in my paper. But I'm always gonna be thinking about what [artist] Frank Ocean is doing next, I'ma go check on this blog and things like that, so it's like, I wanna just invest everything I'm

saying and all the thoughts I have into this paper and if I don't there's no need to really plagiarize.

Jonathan described how his interest in the subject matter bolstered his confidence and helped him invest in the writing process, allowing him to know himself better as a writer and recognize writing as a process. He confessed:

> So like reading and writing are actually two of the subjects that I don't enjoy the most, and especially writing, because I get really bad writer's block when I do write academically, but in terms of social media, that's mainly where I write...[But now] I don't really see myself as that horrible of a writer any more...I guess my confidence kinda grew....I feel like this time around I actually felt as if I, in all aspects of my topic, I knew exactly what I was talking about. 'Cause sometimes...I don't really understand all of the elements fully, so it's like, eerrhhh, I'm kind of confused on the situation but I don't have time to discuss it or research it anymore.

Martin, a freshman, described how reflecting on his everyday literacies in a literacy narrative assignment built his confidence. He said:

> I got to college thinking that these classes are going to be really hard, I'm not that well of a writer, and then ...when you told us to write a blog [about our personal literacies], I really enjoyed writing the blog, so once I started writing the blog, my confidence in writing just grew more....As a kid I never really liked reading. I was always, whenever they would ask me to read something in school, like, "Read this book," it was always like I had to do it for school, I would never do it on my own....But then, when we did the literacy [unit] I realized I've been reading magazines my whole life. I actually have been reading, I am reading, I just never saw it as reading because it's something I really enjoyed.

Martin's comments highlighted the ways that new literacies pedagogies that acknowledge everyday acts of reading and writing build student confidence. Other student commentary indicated the anti-racism inherent in recognizing a range of everyday literacies. Martin connected learning about hiphop sampling practices to his own uptake of advanced argumentation techniques.

> Sometimes in my text that's what I often do, use older texts and, then I source them, and then I use something that I've written before, I use it into a new essay that I have to write, or something that I read from, I base my work off of that, to make it better....Yeah, and every time I listen to a song, I'm like, Oh, sampling!

My colleague's student Ruth, a Black woman, specifically associated the course's appeal with its multimodal curriculum and the heavy presence of music. She told me, "it was nice to come to class and not be given something to read every time but you're listening to the music or he's playing music while you're talking and then you're starting to get a feel for hiphop —I'll say it was very relaxing." For Ruth, an International Relations major, the same feelings that engaged her in class were what made hiphop universal. Reflecting on her research project on hiphop in the Arab Spring, she described sharing a song she was researching with a friend:

> I had a friend last night listen to one of the songs that I was listening to, can't understand what it's saying but it has such a nice beat and it's one of those songs like it's the beats that I associate with that feeling [of] hip-hop and so she was listening to it – she's like *this is nice* and I'm like *right* and I even – it's a song for the revolution telling people to – *the revolution has just begun, long live Egypt* and all this stuff but she just listening to the beat even if I didn't see that, just the beat, you know, already has me…

Ruth's classmate Rachel reiterated the power of music to engage students. "There's something to the way a song makes you feel when you hear it" that engages students in a way written texts can't.

My student Anum echoed the importance of the course's relevance to her learning. She told me,

> I loved it…It really made it seem as if we were learning about modern events or current events that happened and instead of just sitting down and reading or analyzing lyrics from songs, it was more about what we thought about the world outside of that class, does that make sense?

For Anum, having hiphop in the classroom helped her feel understood. Professors, she told me, "they don't come from the same environment as you did…they had way more than you did…the majority of them will probably not have the same connection as artists or rappers will, you know?" This identification with course material carried Anum through a difficult writing process. "It took me like at least 6 or 7 hours sitting down just to find out what I was trying to say and…I decided to just list out all the sources that I had and find out what was in common with them…so it took a lot but I finally narrowed it down to like a main point, which was hard to do…it was very time consuming." Interestingly, Anum, who identified herself as a major hiphop fan, located hiphop's ability to ground student identification and investment in the neoliberal scripts of overcoming or bootstrapping that were inherent in the music. She told me,

> That's why I love Eminem is because he brings up his past and tells people that this is what I had…I had less than you have and I came out to be this successful so if you have this then you can be even more successful…It lets them know that these rappers are with you and they know how you feel and they're rooting for you to be able to achieve whatever you can. I think that's why people relate to hiphop is because they know that message and they just keep going for it.

This statement highlights the contradictory nature of hiphop as the subject of a liberatory pedagogy. Hiphop motivates students and can scaffold critical learning even as it often reinscribes dominant discourses like the hegemonic American notion that hard work is always meritocratically rewarded rather than that opportunity is structured by systems of racism, sexism, and empire.

Interest and identification with course materials helped students invest in close reading in class work and beyond, pushing past ambient anti-Blackness that dismissed hiphop music's value. Chrissy, a white woman, explained that learning to listen to music more closely "taught me a lot...like not judging right away, not just skimming the surface, you know, like looking a little bit more deeper into different things." Multiple students from both my colleague's and my own classes said that their critical engagement with music in the course had changed how they listened to music on their own. Rob told me, "before this class it was kind of, like, bobbing my head, like listening in my car, but now I like to listen to it—and understand it—more than just, bounce to it." Chrissy told me that although people think "hiphop is ignorant," she found that "as we picked apart pieces of the songs, you realized that they have a lot more meaning." Although Chrissy was a longtime hiphop and R&B fan, she described being called an "Oreo" and a "forty-year-old Black man in a white woman's body" by her white female friends for preferring rap and R&B to the pop music they liked. However, she still believed that "even though people say that rap is like just talking and yelling, I think that like those two types of music [rap and R&B] you honestly have to have the most talent for." A white male student, Dan, shared similar experiences, commenting that "my friends always made fun of me...for listening to too hard of rap...and my parents were always against it whenever I played it in the car they'd always be like all this foul language, how do you listen to this."

Neither my courses nor my colleague's sufficiently taught sociolinguistic approaches to AAVE. The lingering hiphop illiteracies in student exit interviews demonstrate that hiphop discourse must be taught sociolinguistically to combat pervasive linguistic racism. Even my students who read texts on Black English by Smitherman lacked a deep understanding of AAVE as a grammatical language that is perceived socially as low-prestige, but is not intrinsically inferior to white mainstream English (Baker-Bell), demonstrating that these key concepts were not sufficiently prioritized in class. Anum clarified how anti-Blackness leads to discrimination against the Black Language practices of rappers. She referenced our class discussion of Kanye West's song "We Don't Care," in which I drew attention to West's choice to use the Black Language structure of the zero copula (Baker-Bell, 76) in his affirmation "We smart." She told me:

> So, I didn't really think about this before this class that a lot of the lyrics from like Black English is—it's not really known as grammar. It's usually known as Black people can't or they can't—they're not as literate as white people are or people in the society and it really opened my eyes trying to figure out that they are—they are literate, they just choose to make it their own language to speak out to the um—they try to make a message out to society and I thought that was—I didn't really think about that before this class.

This statement reflects a developing, but still shallow, recognition of the value of Black Language that misses its own rule-following grammaticality. For David, a white freshman, learning about language varieties laid the foundation for him to listen to and really *hear* minoritized speakers in the future.

> We talked about the way [Jay-Z] spelled something [in his memoir], and how most academics wouldn't like ever think to teach that type of lyric or that artist just cause of the way he spelled—I think he spelled "cuz" like "c-u-z" when it was really supposed to be "because." And I made the point in class that we wouldn't, we would probably overlook that a lot of the times... [But now] I don't really care if something is spelled wrong as long as I can find meaning in it for myself, and I think others can too . . . Just because it's spelled wrong I don't think changes the validity of it.

David's comments here crucially mirror that, in our society, speech in minoritized language varieties can be dismissed on an epistemic level: *invalid*. This moment and others brought home the stakes of my need to shift my pedagogy to make sure students understood language diversity, language prestige and subordination, and linguistic racism, since, like Anum, David still is referring to Black Language practices as "wrong." Jonathan affirmed that learning about BL helped him make sense of why he was always told as a kid "that I talk very white." Not learning about varieties of English had confused him as a child, and even learning about AAVE without lessons on language prestige didn't give him a full vocabulary for understanding the conflicting linguistic messaging he received. He said, "that always confused me cause, I always saw it as I'm speaking proper, but like, to say I'm not speaking Black enough, is kind of um, well not kind of, it's very insulting, and to connect improper speech with Black dialect is very, kind of, annoying, I guess, to say." My class gave Jonathan space, but insufficient conceptual grounding, to discuss his linguistic upbringing.

These conversations occurred in the context of the nationally and locally emerging Black Lives Matter Movement and protests against police and vigilante killings of Black people. Tamika, a Black woman, told me that she was glad to explore issues of racial injustice in class, especially since "this whole year has been like not overly shitty but like more shitty for African Americans than in the past." "I have a brother, I have like a young like Black cousin," she told me, and "this class is definitely a good way for me to like incorporate my culture and my identity and my beliefs into my paper." Chrissy, who was white, told me that while it was hard to talk about race in class, current events had brought racial politics to the fore.

> The main issue is kind of just brushed aside until as of recent with all these riots and everything…I feel like even in class it's like too heavy of a subject if someone is African American in the class, it's just a really, really touchy subject to talk about in a classroom with people you don't know so you don't know how you're gonna offend somebody and especially like if our professor's African American.

Chrissy's white classmate Sarah echoed the sense of fear she believed white students felt around saying the wrong thing. For Sarah, who felt a lifelong awareness of racial injustice, she was thrilled to see the class open to these discussions, telling me, "I loved it."

> I think it needs to happen more in every class, in every possible way. I just think that the problem is that a lot of people are afraid of talking about it,

and it's a sensitive topic so people dance around it. But it's a topic that really needs to be addressed… especially with things like police violence and all the shootings that have been happening, it's really important to address things like that and this is still the only class that I've ever taken that's really like looked at what is happening right now and how it relates to other contemporary things like the music of right now…by being in a class that's willing to talk about it, um, I think you sort of just become more comfortable with the language surrounding it and being able to talk about it yourself and being more educated about it, so, I think it's really important. I liked it.

Chrissy and Sarah's valuing of forthrightness in my colleague's courses was echoed by Yetunde, a Black student in my sophomore class. But while Yetunde echoed the value of these conversations, she also felt more tension around racially charged moments in class. And while Sarah and Chrissy were happy and excited to be discussing race, Yetunde gestured toward the ways that, at least in my course, class was still too oriented around white students' learnings and needs. She said:

> I just remember like moments in class where it was like really tense because people were talking about um, things that kind of – people don't like to talk about, but it was okay because it was in the text and it was part of the assignment, so like you could tell like they were uncomfortable, but they really want to say it so they were like really – you know you felt like the energy coming from them.

But Yetunde qualified her affirmation, locating herself at a remove from the conversation:

> I wasn't glad that they were like siding with me because I'm an African American woman and this text promotes the culture that I'm supposed to identify with…but I was happy that they were like being honest with themselves about how they felt about it, you know? And not really being afraid to express that, so it wasn't – it wasn't moments about me, but more about I'm glad that I'm here with other people as they're getting through that, like they're working through that.

Yetunde's classmate Courtney, a Native American student, also saw white students dominating class discussion. "A lot of the male white students did express their views more so than anyone else. I don't know if that means they connected more with it or if they had more ideas, but they definitely do have some level of um, connection to it." The difference between Yetunde and Courtney's comments versus Chrissy and Sarah's comments taught me that class discussions were still too oriented around white students' coming to awareness and that I needed to find new strategies to center the learning and knowledge of Black students and students of color.

Their classmate Jonathan thought my class could have gone much farther in using hiphop to confront not just national but campus racism and segregation. He told me,

> Hiphop is actually a thing that can like unify students, because it's something that we all indulge in, especially because coming from [CNYU], it is like a known thing across the campus that we're like sort of self-segregated? So like, knowing what I guess the Black community takes so personal as hiphop is something that we could possibly share with every other culture on this campus as like unifying a topic of interest, and bring it to our discussions in class, and out of class... 'Cause one of the things about hiphop is it's kind of an art of truth in things, and one of the truths of [CNYU] is the climate our campus has, and discussing the type of environment we live in would be I think beneficial for everyone...and I think throwing in things like the hyper-sexualized activities and drugs and things, things that like hiphop are always mentioning, throwing those in there as well, cause again that's like another issue or topics that [Central] students can relate to.

In this comment, Jonathan breaks through the stereotypes that criminalize Black and brown youths while white students engage in the same behaviors with impunity, by ascribing the drug and alcohol abuse and sexual violence normally associated with hiphop texts to behaviors he witnessed on his elite PWI campus. Jonathan saw hiphop in the classroom as an opportunity to confront and repair campus harms.

For me, the stakes of this work were most apparent in a conversation with Ruth, a Black woman who had not been one of my students. The daughter of a conservative Black mother, Ruth shared with me deep feelings of inadequacy and fear. Her comments showed the ways that hiphop pedagogy can give students space to unpack the emotions and ideologies that shape their attitudes about learning. After asking me for advice about graduate school, Ruth told me,

> That's good, because I'm like sitting here frightened about the future...One of the things that I realize in my life is that I haven't really accomplished a lot, I don't think I really earned a lot, so sometimes I doubt my own abilities, like sometimes opportunities especially from where I come from, they're presented to you and you do have to compete for it just a little bit, but you know you don't have to compete for it that much, so you get put into positions you do things, but I don't know if I really had the skills to do well with those, so I always question my writing, question everything, my own abilities....

Describing her enjoyment listening to Kendrick Lamar, who critiqued white supremacy while also demanding personal responsibility from his Black listeners, she told me,

> My mom, you know, she was not – she's not – I don't wanna say she's not a African American supporter, but she's always on the side of the argument you know take responsibility and that's kind of how I've grown up and you know I debate with my mom back and forth cause I think like she's a little too conservative, like ma you have to acknowledge some of the systems of oppression too—and this is something she always does is like oh, those – that person did this, that person all right they're not doing this, well I go mom there're also other reasons behind why certain things are you know so-

cial economics you know it's different things, but I will say this, I did appreciate you know listening to artists who took a different stance, like took that responsibility stance.

Ruth's comments highlight for me how hiphop is a source of contradictory commodity products that can both "retain the mass-mediated spotlight on the cultural stage and at the same time function as a voice of social critique and criticism" (Rose 101). Hiphop's mass-marketed ubiquity makes it a powerful entry point for student learning, but we must go further than hiphop products when teaching research-backed concepts. Thus, while hiphop culture offers a space where students can negotiate the ways ideologies shape their lives on the level of the affective, Ruth's comments also show that she needs her courses to teach her *content* about these "systems of oppression," so she can gain not just space but *concepts* with which to understand her world. For writing instructors, these lessons should focus on how power functions through language. In these student interviews, we hear students working to fit their writing classes into their efforts to be successful, making judgments about writing courses' worth, making decisions about how much energy, time, and effort to invest in the study of writing, and balancing their individualized efforts to be successful in a world that has foreclosed opportunities for their generation, with their efforts to incorporate radical knowledge and build practices of solidarity on campus and beyond.

Outro: Confronting My Own Hiphop Illiteracies

Conducting this study led me to significantly revise my pedagogy. These conversations taught me, a white teacher who had insufficiently named and combatted whiteness in my classrooms, that hiphop does not automatically produce an anti-racist or radical curriculum, but rather that hiphop's contradictory messages and ideologies themselves need to be interrogated with key theoretical tools from literacy studies, sociolinguistics, and women's and gender studies. In order to engage hiphop culture more responsibly in my current course "Hiphop, Orality, and Language Diversity," I open class with texts on hiphop and English language variety. I teach that AAVE is a grammatical, rule-following language whose low prestige is a function of hegemonic American anti-Blackness, not any inherent inferiority of the language.

Noting the dominance of male voices in my course discussions and on my syllabi, I also reoriented my course materials to feature Black women and women of color artists and scholars. We open class by watching Jamila Lysicott's slam poem on dialect diversity, "3 Ways to Speak English," and build to three key readings: the first chapter of Richardson's *Hiphop Literacies;* the third chapter of Tricia Rose's *Black Noise*, on the Afrodiasporic roots of hiphop's beats and samples; and DJ Lynnée Denise's article "The Afterlife of Aretha Franklin's 'Rock Steady': A Case Study in DJ Scholarship," in which Denise autoethnographically theorizes her DJ practitioner knowledge as "erasure resistance" (64) that affirmatively curates Black queer and women musicians into rotation.

Instead of analyzing music by male artists, I focus our attention on female rappers like Cardi B, Chika, and Noname. I have also become much more reflexive in identifying myself as a white mainstream English speaker, and I use reflective and reflexive writing prompts to invite students to self-identify, articulate their own language practices, and reflect on the ethical implications of their similarity or difference with the communities they are studying in their research.

Reflexivity brings forward the true diversity in the room; helps all students, including non-Black people of color, self-identify; and helps students connect to their passions and communities when researching. As a result, our class's research has gone global, multilingual, and feminist-forward. While hiphop's brilliance and viral appeal makes it an ideal vehicle for teaching students about writing, language, and literacy, this study shows that anti-Blackness can only be sufficiently understood and combatted in hiphop literacy classrooms at PWIs when students are offered critically reflexive literacy concepts, tools, and practices.

Works Cited

@2Chainz. "[Central New York] University was a Movie." Instagram post. 25 April 2014. https://www.instagram.com/p/nO_OUSTYX9/?utm_source=ig_embed&ig_rid=a6678fb6-6391-47f2-813a-2155d6aa7c44

Alim, H. Samy. "Creating 'An Empire Within an Empire': Critical Hip Hop Language Pedagogies and the Role of Sociolinguistics." *Global Linguistic Flows: Hip Hop Cultures, Youth Identities, and the Politics of Language.* Ed. H. Samy Alim, Awad Ibrahim, and Alastair Pennycook. New York: Routledge, 2009: 213-30.

Anson, Chris M. "Response and the Social Construction of Error." *Assessing Writing 7* (2000): 5-21.

Baker-Bell, April. *Linguistic Justice.* Routledge, 2020.

Ball, Arnetha and Pamela Ellis. "Identity and the Writing of Culturally and Linguistically Diverse Students." *Handbook of Research on Writing: Society, School, Individual, Text.* Lawrence Erlbaum Associates, 2007: 499-513.

Banks, Adam. *Digital Griots: African American Rhetoric in a Multimedia Age.* Southern Illinois UP, 2011.

Bonilla-Silva, Eduardo. *Racism Without Racists: Color-Blind Racism & Racial Inequality in Contemporary America.* Rowman & Littlefield Publishers, Inc., 2010.

Brandt, Deborah. "Sponsors of Literacy." *Writing About Writing: A College Reader,* Ed. Douglas Downs and Elizabeth Wardle. New York: Bedford/St. Martin's, 2014: 331-352.

Brown, Ruth Nicole. *Black Girlhood Celebration: Toward a Hip-hop Feminist Pedagogy.* Peter Lang, 2009.

Brown, Tessa. "'Let the People Rap!' Cultural Rhetorics Pedagogy and Practices under CUNY's Open Admissions, 1968–1978." *Journal of Basic Writing,* 39.1 (2019): pp.106-143

—. "SCHOOLED: Hiphop Composition at the Predominantly White University." Diss., Syracuse U, 2017. https://surface.syr.edu/etd/764.

—. "What Else Do We Know? Translingualism and the History of SRTOL as Threshold Concepts in Our Field." *College Composition and Communication* 71:4 (2020): 591-619.

Carter, Shawn "Jay-Z." *Decoded*. New York: Spiegel & Grau, 2010.

Charmaz, Kathy. *Constructing Grounded Theory: A Practical Guide through Qualitative Analysis*. Sage, 2006.

Craig, Todd and Carmen Kynard. "Sista Girl Rock: Women of Colour and Hip-Hop Deejaying as Raced/Gendered Knowledge and Language." *Changing English* 24.2 (2017): 143-158.

Democratizing Knowledge Collective of Syracuse University. "Syracuse University must further address Hanna Strong incident." *The Daily Orange*. 15 September 2014.

Denise, Lynnée. "The Afterlife of Aretha Franklin's 'Rock Steady': A Case Study in DJ Scholarship." *The Black Scholar* 49.3 (2019): 62-72.

Gee, James Paul. "Literacy, Discourse, and Linguistics: Introduction." *Writing About Writing: A College Reader*, Ed. Douglas Downs and Elizabeth Wardle. New York (2014): Bedford/St. Martin's, 481-497.

Green, Jr., David F. Ed. *Visions and Cypher: Explorations of Literacy, Discourse, and Black Writing Experiences*. Inprint Editions, 2016.

"Hanna Strong." SyracuseFan.com. 6 September 2016. https://syracusefan.com/threads/hanna-strong.79635/page-2

Harris, Joseph. *Rewriting: How to Do Things with Texts*. Logan, UT: Utah State UP, 2006.

Hill, Marc Lamont. *Beats, Rhymes, and Classroom Life: Hip Hop Pedagogy and the Politics of Identity*. Teachers College Press, 2009.

Howard, Rebecca Moore, Tricia Serviss, and Tanya K. Rodrigue. "Writing from Sources, Writing from Sentences." *Writing and Pedagogy* 2.2 (2010): 177-192.

Hunter, Margaret L. and Kimberly D. Nettles. "What about the White Women?: Racial Politics in a Women's Studies Classroom." *Teaching Sociology* 27 (1999): 385-397.

Hurt, Byron, dir. "Barack & Curtis: Manhood, Power, and Respect." Bhurt.com, 2008.

Ivanić, Roz. *Writing and Identity: The Discoursal Construction of Identity in Academic Writing*. John Benjamins, 1998.

Jordan, June. "Nobody Mean More to Me than You and the Future Life of Willie Jordan." *Reading Culture: Contexts for Critical Reading and Writing*. Eds. Diana George and John Trimbur. Pearson Longman, 2007 pp.160-169.

Jordan, Zandra L. "Students' Rights, African American English, and Writing Assessment: Considering the HBCU." *Race and Assessment*. Ed. Asao B. Inoue and Mya Poe. New York: Peter Lang Publishing, Inc., 2012, pp. 97-109.

Judy, R.A.T. "On the Question of [N***a] Authenticity." *That's the Joint! The Hip-Hop Studies Reader*. Ed. Forman and Neal. 2nd ed. Routledge, 2012:

Kirkland, David E. "'The Rose that Grew from Concrete": Postmodern Blackness and New English Education." *The English Journal* 97.5 (2008): 69-75.

Kirsch, Gesa E. and Joy S. Ritchie. "Theorizing a Politics of Location in Composition Studies." *College Composition and Communication* 46.1 (1995): 7-29.

Kitwana, Bakari. *Why White Kids Love Hip Hop: Wankstas, Wiggers, Wannabes, and the New Reality of Race in America.* Basic Civitas Books, 2005.

Lamar, Kendrick. *To Pimp A Butterfly.* TDE/ Aftermath/ Interscope Records, 2015.

Lindsey, Treva. "Let Me Blow Your Mind: Hip Hop Feminist Futures in Theory and Praxis," *Urban Education* 50.1 (2015): 52-77.

Lorenz, Taylor. "The Original Renegade." *The New York Times*. 13 February 2020. https://www.nytimes.com/2020/02/13/style/the-original-renegade.html

Love, Bettina L. *Hip Hop's Li'l Sistas Speak: Negotiating Hip Hop Identities and Politics in the New South.* Peter Lang, 2012.

Lysicott, Jamila. "3 Ways to Speak English." *Ted*. Youtube video. https://www.youtube.com/watch?v=k9fmJ5xQ_mc

Nowacek, Rebecca S. *Agents of Integration: Understanding Transfer as a Rhetorical Act.* Southern Illinois UP, 2011.

Parham, Jason. "TikTok and the Evolution of Digital Blackface." *Wired*. 4 August 2020. https://www.wired.com/story/tiktok-evolution-digital-blackface/

Richardson, Elaine. *Hiphop Literacies.* Routledge, 2006.

Rose, Tricia. *Black Nose: Rap Music and Black Culture in Contemporary America.* Wesleyan University Press, 1994.

Sanfiorenzo, Dimas. "Hip-Hop Is Officially the Most Popular Genre in the United States." *Okayplayer*. Web.

Saldaña, Johnny. *The Coding Manual for Qualitative Researchers*. 2nd ed. Sage, 2013.

Samuels, Brett. "#SpeakUpSU forum provides space to discuss campus diversity issues in wake of Hanna Strong video." *The Daily Orange*. 15 September 2014.

Semuels, Alana. "How to Decimate a City." *The Atlantic*. 20 November 2015. https://www.theatlantic.com/business/archive/2015/11/syracuse-slums/416892/

Silver, Tony, dir. *Style Wars*. Prod. Henry Chalfant. Public Art Films. 1983

Smitherman, Geneva. *Word from the Mother: Language and African Americans.* Routledge, 2006.

Sobande, Francesca. Spectacularized and Branded Digital (Re)presentations of Black People and Blackness. *Television & New Media* 22.2 (2021): 131-146.

Street, Brian. "What's 'New' in New Literacy Studies? Critical Approaches to Literacy in Theory and Practice. *Current Issues in Comparative Education*, vol. 5, no. 2, 2003, pp. 77–91.

"Students' Right to Their Own Language." *College Composition and Communication* 25 (1974): 1-65. NCTE. Web. 13 March 2015.

Young, Vershawn Ashanti, Rusty Barrett, Y'Shanda Young-Rivera, and Kim Brian Lovejoy. *Other People's English: Code-Meshing, Code-Switching, and African American Literacy*. Teachers' College Press, 2014.

Yousman, Bill. "Blackophilia and Blackophobia: White Youth, the Consumption of Rap Music, and White Supremacy." *Communication Theory* 13.4 (2006): 366-391.

Author Bio

Tessa Brown, Ph.D. is currently on leave from her position as Lecturer in the Program in Writing and Rhetoric at Stanford University, where she was the founding advisor of *The Word: The Stanford Journal of Student Hiphop Research* (open to submissions from college students at any school!). Her scholarship has appeared in *College Composition and Communication*, the *Journal of Basic Writing*, *Peitho*, and *Composition Studies*, and her fiction, essays, and reviews have appeared in *Harper's*, *Hyperallergic*, the *Los Angeles Review of Books*, and elsewhere. TessaBrown@Stanford.edu

From the Book and New Media Review Editor's Desk

Jessica Shumake, Editor
University of Notre Dame

Stephen M. North laments that few others in rhetoric and composition share his sense of urgency regarding the genre of the book review and opines that book reviews, at their apogee, are "the occasion for vital, visible, memorable exchanges: the print equivalent, say, of the salon and/or the street corner, current and accessible" (349). Beyond being informative and evaluative, North states that reviews "give new voices a chance to be heard" (352). Further, North articulates that the book review is an uncertain genre because the writer's audience is invisible in the sense that when reviewers write almost always *no one writes back*. In my capacity as an editor, I have, on occasion, heard back from authors who praise a reviewer's careful reading, kindness, or thoroughness. I have also fielded legitimate grievances over misspelled names in an edited collection, which even my scrupulous attention to detail missed and which required an erratum. Overall, North's observation that there is a lack of public authorial commentary on book reviews holds true. Furthermore, North sees the purpose of book reviews as an open question: are reviewers helping readers understand *how* to read a book or helping them *decide* whether or not to read it at all?

My purpose, in this issue, is to invite readers to find thought-provoking books to read. The six reviews assembled here span and traverse the following capacious domains: building literacy initiatives that center oral conversations and community needs; finding pleasure in shared family reading activities with young children; transnational feminist theory and activism; critical pedagogy, liberal arts education, and literacy learning in prison classrooms; queer rhetorical counter-literacy practices; and feminist historiography and literacy sponsorship. There is much reading delight to be had here and I hope these reviews open up possibilities for new thought to practitioners, students, activists, and scholars alike working in any area of community writing.

Works Cited

North, Stephen M. "On Book Reviews in Rhetoric and Composition." *Rhetoric Review* 10.2 (1992): 348–363.

Literacy as Conversation: Learning Networks in Urban and Rural Communities

Eli Goldblatt and David A. Jolliffe
University of Pittsburgh Press, 2020, pp. 216

Reviewed by Rachel E.H. Edwards
Temple University

In *Literacy as Conversation: Learning Networks in Urban and Rural Communities* Eli Goldblatt and David A. Jolliffe introduce their literacy-based, definition expanding, and conversational networking approach to giving marginalized urban and rural communities room to mold the literate practices that will improve their real conditions so there are greater possibilities for educational, economic, and political advancement. They purposely invite a wider audience to consider alternate forms of literacy learning outside school settings to stimulate the expansion of a network of supporters. Goldblatt and Jolliffe identify these supporters as potentially consisting of the individuals, non-profit organizations, and philanthropic extensions of for-profit corporations they have encountered when building literacy-based initiatives in the neighborhoods and regions surrounding Temple University and University of Arkansas. They also show that without networking done to connect these entities, the various programs, and projects they discuss will continue to fall short of extending the growth of literacies in these communities that improve access to educational, health and human services. What makes this book captivating and convincing is the sheer length and breadth of the combined experiences Goldblatt and Jolliffe draw on and the conversational style they use to expound upon and speculate about the types of literacy that can be practiced to make specific community needs visible and addressable. The work Goldblatt and Jolliffe do to illuminate and express the ignored experiences and enrich the lives of those whose literate learning must grow out of debris-strewn city medians or overly saturated farm soil—relegated now to growing economic prospects for industry—is indeed important and inspiring. As intended, *Literacy as Conversation* infused me, as it will other readers, with a new or renewed commitment to incorporating out-of-school literacy learning into my work as a teacher, researcher, and community member because it concretely serves those underserved by the academy thus far.

In "Part I: Introducing Our Terms," Goldblatt and Jolliffe layout how their conversational approach rests on their conceptions of literacy and learning networks. They position themselves as working from a New Literacy Studies orientation and primarily rely on Deborah Brandt's conceptions of literacy and sponsorship for their inter-relationally oriented definitions. They define literacy as continued conversations between disenfranchised people who are seeking to take action to improve their situations (7). They define learning networks as interconnected public, non-profit and private sponsors whose resources enable local plans for literacy-based actions to come to fruition (8). Goldblatt then introduces the framework of analysis he calls the Literacy Education Audit of Resources (LEARN) as the way audience members can contemplate the resources offered by sponsors in relation to the needs in areas surrounding universities so they can be connected to enrich material conditions and opportunities. As Goldblatt and Joliffe begin to enact LEARN by assessing needs in their respective locales, they indicate they will be constantly pushing against school-based, public, and civic conceptions of literacy as basic acts of reading or writing externally motivated by pressures to meet educational grading or testing standards. Additionally, Goldblatt and Jolliffe establish they will demonstrate how intrinsically motivated literate acts in communities lead to tangible products or changes through exploring the way meaning, conversations, and utterances unfold *in situ*. Goldblatt and Jolliffe understand "live and unfolding meanings" as evolving understandings of real situational climates and exigencies that stem from speaking and working with the people who are experiencing them (15–17). They describe locations where shared language and literacies are formed, acquired, and learned to be practiced through joining others to take purposeful, collaborative actions within a local context that serve aesthetic or pragmatic needs as spaces for "multiple conversations" (15–18). For the authors, literate acts are anchored to both "oral and interior utterances" because they can be tied to externalized versions of thought influenced by understandings produced within and realized through texts that create social connections and galvanize reformation (15–21). Ultimately, Goldblatt and Jolliffe convey that they believe their LEARN framework will only bring funders together to support communal literate acts if understanding is built about how they serve a given community's needs for social, political, and economic mobility.

It should be noted that Goldblatt and Jolliffe end the first part of the book by simulating an actual conversation between them that directly attends to the charged issue of their positionality as white, highly educated males writing about literacies in culturally and racially different communities. They articulate that their aim in the book and throughout their careers has been to use their power and privilege to assist communities in using literate acts to fulfill their own agendas. Nothing supports their claim more than their book's privileging of oral conversation as a valid and valuable tool for literacy—especially for groups whose oral cultural practices have continually been discounted within and outside the academy as legitimate forms of literacy.

In the next two parts, Goldblatt and Jolliffe narrate their own experiences and share observations about how exactly these new literacy characteristics were used to actively respond to the specific educational, economic, political, and social constellation of needs of communities within Philadelphia and Arkansas. Moreover, they give us a glimpse into the sources of tensions and connections between participants and learning networks of literacy sponsorship and how they impact outcomes. These portraits and conversations are intended to engage readers in thinking and talking about how these insights can be applied to build learning networks that fund and advance necessary literacy efforts of communities surrounding campuses.

Goldblatt's chapters in "Part II: Learning Networks in Philadelphia" masterfully blend narrative-based and theoretical reflection to provide illustrative lessons about how the nuanced dialogues that do or do not occur between learning networks and the members of the community steered the directions or conclusions of out-of-school, community arts, and urban farm-based literacy programs and projects. Since Goldblatt's experiences with possessing or seeking funding vary, he attends to the choices leaders make to accrue necessary funding that can cause intentions to serve the actual needs and concerns of neighborhoods through community organizing to fall to the wayside. In other words, the costs of not attending to "live and unfolding meanings" revealed through "multiple conversations" within organizations whose literacy objectives fall into traditional and untraditional categories are cogently portrayed. Goldblatt's story about an endeavor focused on providing avenues for emotional release and beautification through cultivating artistic literacies in North Philadelphia sponsored by the Village of Arts and Humanities are memorable and enlightening in this way. What Goldblatt communicates is how the Village became misguided in their mission to artistically represent and address African American urban trauma when they hired an African artist and a counselor who pushed their own visions of what trauma looked like and healing meant. He hints that if the Village asked for community members' input about the project's design, message and creation, their collective creative literacies could have been used to form exquisite expressions of the neighborhood's sources of pain and reduced poverty-related trauma by providing steady employment. Goldblatt also notably recommends in the city where competition for funding is fierce due to the vast array of organizations serving individual neighborhoods, forming learning networks is critical so funding and experienced volunteers can be shared or developed to increase the possibilities for literacies to thrive throughout the city.

Jolliffe's chapters in "Part III: Learning Networks in Arkansas" stress how learning networks provided the human capital for his projects that concentrate on using performative literacy practices with local residents, prisoners, and students to improve the health and outlook for educational access, activism, and the economy of inhabitants throughout the state. Since Jolliffe's projects were funded at least in part by his endowed Brown Chair of Literacy position, he emphasizes how conversations between individuals within university and resident organizational sponsors can uncover the talents, mutual commitments, and connections that make select goals attainable. Moreover, he highlights how individuals can coalesce to change how populaces are seen and see themselves as literate creators whose output garners movements that resist institutional political agendas. What I find compelling is Jolliffe's notion that dramatic texts—including poems—embody a person's "oral" and usually hidden "interior utterances" so that reading, writing responses to, and performing them invites empathetic identification with and fosters novel understandings of the author's contextual experiences. For the networks of students, prisoners, writers, actors, and educators in Jolliffe's accounts who elicit, create, and perform dramatic texts and audiences who witness these performances, both these identifications and understandings cement communal bonds as well as stimulate literate growth and political activism. Jolliffe's sharing of the mostly African American death row inmates' representative responses to Prison Story Project prompts that inspired the creation of the play *On the Row* best shows how "oral and interior utterances" are literate acts that can spark reformation of public identities and political decisions through performance. Initially, as one of the prisoners, Brandon, observes in the play's epilogue, these responses challenged prisoners' assumptions about the monstrousness of their fellow inmates and showed them, "our humanity; our worth. That we have something to offer too. We too matter, no matter what horrible things we did (or didn't do) in the past to land us on death row" (178–179). After Governor Asa Hutchinson announced that eight death row inmates would be executed in eleven days, four of whom contributed to the project, these poignant responses fueled public efforts to stop the executions and do away with the death penalty as the play was performed in venues across and outside the state. Jolliffe and his Prison Story Project team decided to continue to perform *On the Row* in defiance of Arkansas Department of Corrections efforts to suppress these prisoner's voices by withdrawing their permission for its public performance. In the end, two of these four inmate participants received stays of execution.

In their conclusion, Goldblatt and Jolliffe return to their LEARN framework and model how it can be used to generate literacy initiatives through learning networks of support. They more fully assess needs within Philadelphia and Arkansas by examining and comparing population, diversity, economic, educational climate, and financial resources and determine these factors converge to limit access to college or vocational training in the city and the country. Due to this assessment, they conclude that there is an overall need for degrees and training so individuals in both places have the knowledge, credentials, and skills necessary to accrue economic rewards in the United States and, therefore, the status to effectively band together to gain political traction on issues that impact how they live. In light of these needs, Goldblatt and Jolliffe providing practical advice and insight about how to connect these communities with learning networks that amass both money and human resources to address these needs. What becomes clear is that Goldblatt and Jolliffe's efforts to redefine literacy as conversations that lead to actions through learning network financing can bolster community and economic growth for black, brown, ethnic, and poor people. They provide hope that these possibilities for better living conditions will still be made available despite school district, policy maker, and academic institutional neglect.

As a researcher and educator, I find this ending markedly fitting as Asao Inoue and others have brought to the fore questions about how we leverage our power in the academy as composition and rhetoric professionals to make the culture and language of people of color a central part of the conversation so we can begin to understand and change our white habits of practicing and judging writing in the academy. Goldblatt and Jolliffe show us one way to leverage white academic power and privilege by proffering an approach that assesses literate practices according to how much power is accorded to communities of color—or communities with limited financial means—to ensure whatever needs for health, food, shelter, intellectual/creative fulfillment, and life are met.

Works Cited

Inoue, Asao B. "How do we Language so People Stop Killing each Other, Or what do we do about White Language Supremacy?" *College Composition and Communication,* vol. 71, no. 2, 2019, pp. 352–69.

—. "Why I Left the CWPA (Council of Writing Program Administrators). *Asao B. Inoue's Infrequent Words,* 18 Apr. 2021, asaobinoue.blogspot.com/2021/04/why-i-left-cwpa-council-of-writing.html.

Family Literacies: Shared Reading with Young Children

Rachael Levy and Mel Hall
Routledge, 2021, pp.179

Reviewed by Megen Farrow Boyett
University of Louisville

While "family literacy" has been a popular term and concept in para-educational settings since the 1980s, it has often focused on using home life to meet educational aims, rather than studying the family as a site of literate experiences in its own right. In their book *Family Literacies: Reading with Young Children*, Rachael Levy and Mell Hall intentionally move away from school-based aims for pre- and primary-school children to instead ask what *families* get from creating, sustaining, and sharing literacy experiences. They explore a widely acknowledged, but surprisingly under-researched, family literacy practice: reading with young children. Levy and Hall frame what they call "shared reading" as a familial act that shapes routines, reinforces emotional bonds, and displays familial "belonging" both to family members and outsiders. Focusing on children who have not yet started school allows them to explore "shared reading" as a separate activity from "learning to read," though their findings have major implications for both preschool community literacy programs and, potentially, primary classrooms.

The book draws on findings from the Shared Reading Project, which interviews families to understand how shared reading "is perceived in their homes and how it fits (or does not fit) within everyday family life" (13). Levy and Hall's findings stress the importance of understanding the habits and goals of individual families, in order to create programming that supports ongoing literacy practices rather than promoting school readiness. Demonstrating the difference in findings that a shift in focus can yield, the authors examine families and homes, rather than programs, until they discuss implications in the book's final chapters. The authors use theory and methods from sociology to study shared reading as a feature of everyday life, asking what the activity achieves *for families* and making reading a means to an end, rather than a goal.

The book is clearly laid out in ten chapters: an introduction to gaps in family reading research, two chapters reviewing relevant work on reading as a sociological practice and shared reading as a topic of study, one chapter laying out their study's methodological choices and ethical commitments, two chapters discussing findings, two chapters discussing implications, and a conclusion that imagines what shared reading, as defined here, could mean for families once children begin school. The clarity and care of these chapters is a particular strength of *Family Literacies: Reading with Young Children*, at every level of organization. Levy and Hall are careful to explain their interlocutors without heavy theoretical discussions and to make explicit connections between pieces of their study, indicating a desire for findings to be quickly understood and implications quickly put into practice. While this work contributes to family literacy scholarship, it's clear that the authors anticipate practitioners reading and making use of their findings in daily work.

Chapter one, "Reading with Young Children: An Introduction," lays out the central goal of the research study: "to understand what families do when they read with their children," as well as the values, beliefs, and personal choices that inform the practice (9). Previewing the larger conversations of the book, Levy begins with a personal narrative about the importance of shared reading and storytelling in her childhood home. While her own parents neither read on their own nor pushed educational attainment, reading together throughout the day was a treasured activity during her childhood. Using this narrative, the authors invite readers to wonder what motivates parents to read to their children. They focus especially, though not exclusively, on economically disadvantaged families, at whom reading intervention programs are most often aimed.

Having previewed big themes, the writers home in on "reading" and "shared reading" as terms. Drawing from Levy's earlier research with pre- and primary-school children, the authors argue that school discourses couple "reading" with phonetic instruction and mastering skills. When reading was seen as a linear process of learning to de-code print, rather than a meaningful engagement with a text, children as young as kindergarten saw themselves as "poor" readers, or even non-readers. While the authors take it for granted that "most of us want children to become confident, motivated, and engaged readers," they suggest that we must recognize reading as a more fluid construct than traditional school discourse dictates. Studying reading practices within homes—not to "find out what's wrong" but rather "to understand what families do when they read with their children"—offers a way to see reading as a complex set of socio-culturally embedded practices (9). With this in mind, they turn to shared reading, defined as "an activity where a child is engaged in focusing on a text with another person (usually an adult) for a sustained period of time" (9). They define text broadly, to include digital texts and e-readers, though nearly all examples of shared reading within the study were print-based. The authors also clarify that while "shared reading" could mean "reading to a child" or "listening to a child read," the book focuses on the former. Thus, they study the relationship between a caretaking adult and a young child, mediated by a visual text, and distance themselves from studies of reading "mastery." These kinds of careful, expansive definitions—in which the authors specify their use of terms while offering further possibilities for work outside of their own—characterize the book. This sophisticated move invites further work in the same vein, while carving out a niche for this study within family literacy cannon.

In chapter two, "Sociological Perspectives on Reading," Levy and Hall establish the book as primarily a sociological study of reading. Because reading is an everyday practice "deeply embedded in constructions of class, worth, and value," a central purpose of this chapter is to explore how reading functions as a social practice, and how the discourses surrounding it both shape reading practices and people's identities as "readers" (17). They begin by defining "socialization" as an ongoing practice of finding one's identity by interpreting and enacting the values of one's communities. Using Urie Bronfenbrenner's ecological systems theory, they locate school and home as two dominant spheres that children navigate between as they learn to identify and value themselves as "readers." Comparisons between these two spaces helps disrupt an assumption that home literacy experiences should feed into school goals. Instead, they suggest the opposite: Levy's previous play-based research with young readers indicates that a scholastic focus on phonics narrows children's definition of reading and thus their view of themselves as "readers." Homes, on the other hand, seem to provide a broader definition of reading, because members of the family—including children—have an active role in shaping family values and using literacy activities to accomplish their own purposes. Discovering these purposes is a central thrust of the book, but the authors suggest two possibilities: 1) shared reading not only creates physical and emotional bonds between family members and 2) it "displays" the family (broadly defined) as a unit that does "family" things for both members and outsiders. Findings chapters explore how individual families discuss and complicate these two motivations for shared reading.

Chapter three "Shared Reading Practices," acts as a second literature review that brings sociological discussions of literacy into conversation with current research on shared reading practices. Again, the book focuses on adults reading to children, rather than listening to them read, further creating further separation from skill-based perceptions of reading. The authors also re-emphasize children's agency in shared reading activities, which continues to be an important theme in findings. Previous research, they argue, indicates social, emotional, and mental benefits of shared reading for both children and parents. Using "bedtime stories," as an extended example from literature, however, the authors demonstrate that institutional suggestions for shared reading are embedded in socio-cultural discourses of that often privilege white middle-class literacies and require certain material needs to be met. In order to ensure that more families can develop shared reading practices that fit their daily lives, the authors suggest a sustained focus on how and why individual families incorporate reading into their daily routines, as well as barriers they encounter.

In chapter four, "Researching Family Lives," the authors lay out their study constraints and decisions. Unsurprisingly, most work on shared reading has tended to treat children's linguistic development as an end goal—in line with educational outcomes. Diverging from this trend, Levy and Hall emphasize "understanding *families* and their everyday practices" (47, emphasis in original). To this end, they conducted semi-structured narrative interviews in participants' homes, which allowed them to ask about family's routines and shared reading's place within the seemingly mundane practices of everyday life. They also asked about parents' current reading practices and memories of reading as children, to understand whether and how previous associations with reading impacted reading with children (52–53). The twenty-nine parents interviewed are linguistically, racially, educationally and economically diverse, but are all participants in a broader research program called, "Promoting Language Development by Shared Reading." Participation in this research not only created a natural way to invite families into the study but also might have meant that parents were already reflecting on their shared reading practices. Further, it's likely that the types of families participating would either be invited to or voluntarily attend other family literacy programs, even though findings are not meant to be generalizable. In addition to clearly explained study constraints, a merit of this chapter is Levy and Hall's discussion about the ways they occupied "inside" and "outside" positions in conversations with research participants and the ethical considerations they made as a result. Their awareness of power dynamics and their researcher roles is an important reminder of the tenuous space of research and the need for close attention to the interactions between research methodologies and the real people involved.

Chapter five, "Shared Reading as an Everyday Family Practice," is the first of four chapters reporting trends in study findings, all of which focus on how shared reading time currently fits into family life and how families use it to coordinate their days and build bonds. Practically, families use shared reading to solidify their routines and manage aspects of family life. Specific texts are used to support aspects of parenting, such as teaching family values and reinforcing skills like toilet training. Shared reading might help transition to a different activity or type of energy. Relationally, parents use shared reading to build family bonds, a complex process that parents discussed in diverse ways, including through protecting quality time, establishing their parental identity and granting children agency to decide when and how they read. This discussion builds on the idea of displaying "family-ness" through the activities that family members engage in together. In addition to giving quality time, shared reading was also a sensory experience, providing physical closeness that might not have happened without the mediation of a text. The emphasis on using shared reading to accomplish existing family goals, whether maintaining routines or building close bonds, stands in contrast to interventions that want to add in reading time without asking about the individual family's routines or desires.

Chapter six, "Doing and Sustaining Shared Reading; Parents' Aims and Motivations," turns from reading as part of everyday practice to the reasons that parents intentionally make shared reading a habit. The relationship between these two chapters is organic, but chapter six notes the felt benefits that keep parents engaging in shared reading with their children rather than exploring reading within the "pool of activities that make up everyday family life" (82). A significant finding, surprising for the lack of research surrounding it, is parents' focus on the mutual enjoyment found in shared reading times. For some families, and at some times, enjoyment looks like introducing calm and cozy into the wildness of life with toddlers. For others, shared reading tends to be boisterous and energetic, meant to entertain and bring laughter.

Parents consistently reported that 1) they read because they enjoyed the shared time, even if they did not read for pleasure on their own and 2) that if they or their children did not enjoy the time, then they would be less likely engage in it. The enjoyment, then, stems from the atmosphere that shared reading helps to create, and the feedback parents receive from their children, rather than from merely the act of reading itself. For some families, watching their children learn was *part* of receiving positive feedback, but it was not a central motivation. Linguistic development, a central goal in educational programs, is linked with enjoyment, but more like a nice bonus than a motivation. Once again textual engagement serves as a means for creating a certain kind of experience, rather than the goal of the activity. The links between enjoyment, feedback, and to a lesser extent, learning, are key in the following chapters. The intentional ways that Levy and Hall look backward and forward in these finding chapters is useful for researchers, but particularly important for practitioners. The clear scaffolding in these chapters sets up practitioners to align their practices more closely with family motivations.

In chapter seven, "Barriers to Shared Reading," Levy and Hall use findings to extend research identifying what keeps parents from making shared reading a practice. While all but one parent in the Shared Reading Project said that they regularly read with their children, maintaining the habit was not uncomplicated. Seasons of family stress, parents' mental health, and socio-cultural backgrounds that prioritize togetherness, but not necessarily reading, or prioritize education but not reading for pleasure, were all seen to impact habitual engagement in shared reading times. The degree to which barriers impacted shared reading differed from family to family, demonstrating that cultural or class background does not determine a parents' likelihood of reading with their children. On the other hand, families from lower income brackets depended slightly more on positive feedback to continue making reading a habit than did families in higher income brackets. When parents perceived a lack of interest from their children, those from higher income brackets were more likely to push forward, often citing educational reasons, than those from lower income brackets. This is a key takeaway for practitioners and educators hoping to increase reading frequency at home, because the kinds of barriers families list in interviews are less likely to be considered than say, access to reading material, which was not a barrier that any family in the study named. Further, increasing *enjoyment* and *positive feedback* may not be a commonly forwarded goal, but Levy and Hall assert that this is a mistake, given that the affective benefits of shared reading hold much greater appeal than the promise of school readiness. In this chapter, Levy and Hall begin to foreshadow the recommendations in later chapters, while maintaining a focus on the individual family unit. An end goal in asking how shared reading fits into the "minutiae" of everyday life, then, is not simply understanding of how reading fits, but a course correction for practitioners seeking to create interventions that work for a greater variety of families.

While the previous three chapters focus on parents' current relationship with shared reading, chapter eight, "Parents' Relationships with Reading," asks whether past experiences with reading—either in school or families of origin—impacts parents' attitudes toward the activity. The authors particularly wanted to know whether a poor relationship with reading, stemming perhaps from experiences in school, made parents less willing to read with their children. While about a third of parents said they did not enjoy reading for themselves and/or had negative associations with reading as a child, this did not impact their enjoyment of shared reading with their own children. Most of the chapter is focused on this group of parents—who did not read as a child but does read with their own children—in the hopes of finding ways to support current shared reading habits and perhaps help their children continue to enjoy reading. For many of these parents, negative associations stemmed from the narrowed definitions of reading they found in school, struggles with phonics, and memories of being asked to read aloud. With their own children, however, parents did not feel the same pressure to perform and expressed pleasure in the shared experience. Some parents even reported feeling like stronger readers, or finding pleasure reading on their own. Levy and Hall suggest that, following the lead of these families, we should consider *shared reading* as a more expansive concept than mastering language or even gleaning meaning from a text. *Shared reading,* then, includes the sensory and affective aspects of reading as well as the time spent exploring a text. It is often child-led and can move back and forth through the pages of a text, skipping over pages or lingering on pictures. It can even include time spent discussing days or telling stories separate from the physical text, since shared reading often facilitates these moments. While the other findings chapters held fascinating insights, I found this one the most rewarding as a reader. I had a sense that parents were undoing some of the harm that a focus on phonetic mastery and reading schemas had caused, through reading with their children. I found myself hoping, as the next chapter turns to implications, that these study results might answer some of the anxiety over "literacy crises" as educators and program organizers help parents find joy in shared reading without a focus on educational milestones.

Chapter nine, "Working with Families to Promote Shared Reading," turns explicitly to practitioners—including pre-school teachers, literacy program organizers, librarians, social workers, and family therapists—helping families include shared reading in their daily lives. This chapter has a different timbre than the findings chapters. While the four previous chapters drew heavily from sociology to tell the stories of family routines, motivations, and values, this chapter acknowledges that such a study can be used to design better interventions to aid in literacy development. The focus on individual families remains, however, as Levy and Hall remind practitioners that "while they may have expertise in areas related to their own profession, the experts in being in this family are this family" (137). They thus urge practitioners to ask thoughtful questions about a family's daily practices, including reading, and to encourage shared reading work as it is already happening. Linguistic development, they remind, is a side-effect of time spent with texts, but without a cycle of positive feedback families are unlikely to spend their leisure time in shared reading. Because research shows that toddlers and infants benefit from the stimulation of being read to but are less likely than older children to give obviously positive feedback, practitioners are encouraged to help parents expand their concept of engagement. Far from being taught how to read "correctly" with their children, parents may need encouragement that they're doing it right, and a release from educational expectations.

In chapter ten, "Shared Reading and Starting School—A Conclusion" the authors look toward the implications of their findings when children start school. Although the study focuses on shared reading with very young children, school discourse looms large over the rest of the book: Levy and Hall frequently remind us that a phonics focus narrows definitions of what constitutes a "reader," even in early grades, and parents' discussions of their own reading experiences underscores this finding. Thus, an ending chapter focused the study's implications for school age reading helps to ease the sense that the joy of shared reading would necessarily diminish for these families. While the rest of the book has looked at individuals, Levy and Hall here consider what the implications of their study might do to answer educational aims. They point out that a focus on phonics, which narrows "reading" to "de-coding sounds," does very little to help readers analyze whole texts or consider their socio-cultural contexts. Further, as cited throughout the book, narrowed visions of reading can cause some students to think of themselves as "poor readers" discouraging them from engaging further with texts. Thus, while educational institutions have long asked families to partner in meeting *school* goals, Levy and Hall suggest the opposite: that schools might learn from individual families' reading motivations and partner to meet their goals instead. In this and the previous chapter, they encourage practitioners to think of shared reading in terms of "text, talk, time, and togetherness"—a convenient way of summing up family's descriptions of shared reading's benefits to their daily life. Schools and community literacy programs, they suggest, might consider how text facilitates the other three, rather than asking time and togetherness to serve texts.

Family Literacies: Reading with Young Children is an important book for *CLJ* readers because of how often we occupy a liminal space between community members and educational institutions. A lot of community literacy work in education has focused on helping high school and college writers move away from the legacy of school discourses toward thinking of literacy as a complex set of socio-culturally embedded processes. Much less work had examined those youngest of readers and their textual engagement previous to entering classrooms. And yet, given the number of community programs aimed at "school readiness," it's worth asking "how do we design literacy programs that support and encourage families' love of reading on their own terms?" Levy and Hall's book offers insights from their population of families and gives a clear model for gaining insight into families' routines and motivations.

Transnational Feminist Itineraries: Situating Theory and Activist Practice

Ashwini Tambe and Millie Thayer (Eds.)
Duke University Press, 2021. pp. 269

Reviewed by Curtis J. Jewell
Syracuse University

Amidst an increasingly globalized world, abetted by COVID-19 pandemic and its necessitation of online interaction, feminist scholars, activists, and community organizers alike have faced increasing pressures to return their collective focus to more localized struggles. We see this forced movement to the local occur within issues such as reproductive rights in Texas, United States in 2021. Despite this and parallel movements throughout the world, digitally cultivated spaces, as seen in social media platforms, have deepened the possibility for transnational collaboration across borders and boundaries. This collaboration is particularly visible within social justice efforts such as the #BlackLivesMatter movement, which has become a central cry amongst anti-racist movements across the globe. This paradoxical contemporary context created the exigence for *Transnational Feminist Itineraries: Situating Theory and Activist Practice*. Composed for a predominantly academic audience, *Transnational Feminist Itineraries* offers extensive discussions of our contemporary context and how collaborative, feminist practices are being taken up not only within, but across nations.

Transnational Feminist Itineraries is a collaborative collection of essays which aims to contribute to the development of feminist theory and practice through a five-part approach: (1) positing that the global socio-political context requires the tools and methods of transnational feminism; (2) positioning transnational feminism as running parallel, and not in opposition, to other feminist approaches; (3) exploring a historical context rich with cross-border activism; (4) arguing for both the "scaling out" in addition to the "scaling up" of feminist methods; (5) offering critiques of transnational feminism to further complicate the conversation surrounding its place amongst alternative feminisms.

Transnational Feminist Itineraries consists predominantly of case studies. Each chapter takes a unique approach to discussing the affordances of transnational feminism, as well as some of the difficulties engendered within various nations and their relationships across borders. Many of these texts draw on scholars such as the prominent feminist scholar Inderpal Grewal (author of chapter 3); Chandra Talpade Mohanty, known for working across borders and within decolonial frameworks; and Kimberlé Crenshaw, perhaps best known for coining the term intersectionality. While invoking the use of these and other scholars, the authors demonstrate the various contexts within which transnational feminisms offer valuable frames for critiquing and understanding the relationships between and within nations.

Part 1 of *Transnational Feminist Itineraries*, a collection of self-identified provocations, begins with a chapter contributed by the co-editors, Ashwini Tambe and Millie Thayer. Their chapter, "The Many Destinations of Transnational Feminism," situates transnational feminism historically, and illuminates its connections with intersectional and decolonial feminisms. In the chapter, they examine the multiplicity of oppression and question relationships of power—as well as points of divergence, such as transnational feminism's pointed critique of conceptions of nation(alism), intersectional feminism's focus on the intersection of race and gender, and decolonial feminism's critique of the categories and language of scholarship. Tambe and Thayer additionally discuss the importance of "scaling out," creating discussion across ideological boundaries, and critiques such as how transnational feminism is steeped in academic, at times inaccessible language when considering the readers it is crafted for; nonetheless, tangible examples of what conversations might look like outside of academic contexts do not appear within the chapter.

The second chapter of Part 1, "Beyond Antagonism: ReThinking Intersectionality, Transnationalism, and the Women's Studies Academic Job Market" by Jennifer C. Nash, explores how the tailoring of academic job advertisements further separate, and at times confuse, the concepts of intersectionality and transnationalism. Nash focuses on the perception of intersectionality as "a gesture toward complexity" and transnationalism as an ethic of solidarity across difference (43). Within this conceptualization, Nash argues that perceptions of intersectionality range between "an area of focus […] a method or approach […] a cross-cutting theory, method, and practice that supersedes feminist practice" while the term transnational "is treated as a place-based marker and indicates a desire for scholarship that centers non-US locations" (47–49). While Nash's work gives rise to questions about Women's Studies programs' understanding of the relationship between the terms, readers will not find discussions of how job postings connected to the work conducted by the faculty ultimately hired; and whether their dissertations or other scholarly work shared a similar disposition or if the terms were used more as indicators of what was valued in the department than requirements for how the terms needed to be understood by potential candidates. However, Nash clearly articulates a critique of how those within positions of power can determine the discourse's framework.

The concluding chapter of Part 1, "Rethinking Patriarchy and Corruption: Itineraries of US Academic Feminism and Transnational Analysis" by Inderpal Grewal, focuses on the creation of political subjects and how they are constructed in relation to transnational, postcolonial, and intersectional feminisms. While elaborating on the distinctions and similarities between the three positions previously established in the book, Grewal posits transnational feminism as a response to theories of mobility with an intent to "fracture notions of national tradition or culture, or global capitalism and its institutions, as well as hegemonic forms of power" (60). Grewal conducts a case study focusing on the Trump presidency to explore how transnational feminism can be used to understand the construction of empires and "the maintenance of racial patriarchies through privatized accumulation" (62). Grewal's work effectively demonstrates how transnational feminism, while being conceptualized as a theory of elsewhere, can be valuable within US contexts as well.

The initial chapter of Part 2, a triplet addressing issues of scale, begins with "Transnational Feminism and the Politics of Scale: The 2012 Antirape Protests in Delhi" contributed by Srila Roy. Roy's chapter draws upon theorists such as Deleuze and Guattari when discussing the construction of a protest assemblage emerging from the aftermath of the rape and murder of twenty-three-year-old Jyoti Singh Pandey in 2012 Delhi, India (77). The term assemblage captures the unpredictable and multifaceted interactions of both public and private entities engaged with an issue, such as the Delhi events. Roy notes that responses were not uniform, whether demographically or ideologically. Roy provides clarification for readers on the differences between "scaling up" and "scaling out," as these terms are applied to geographically or ideologically diverse constituents. Roy illustrates how movement across boundaries is possible, and thus transnational approaches necessary, even within national borders; furthermore, she offer a discussion of the ever-growing importance of transnational feminism within increasingly divisive political regimes.

Chapter 5, the intermediate section of Part 2, "Transnational Shifts: The World March of Women in Mexico" by Carmen L. Díaz Alba analyzes the World March of Women (WMW) to demonstrate the difficulty of engaging with transnationalism while acknowledging the affordances made on a national level to various organizations. Díaz Alba successfully navigates a standing critique of transnational feminism, the inaccessibility of academically coded language. Without abandoning rigor, Díaz Alba addresses issues of scale and the transitions of responsibilities within organizations as well as other activist concerns such as burnout and the possible disconnect between transnational and local pressures. While the chapter discusses the difficulties of transnational movements, how cross-boundary work is most attainable during moments of international urgency, Díaz Alba also notes how transnational movements such as WMW create spaces for organizations to promote their work who may otherwise not have the necessary resources. Transnational feminism is thus presented as complex, shifting, and always already in a state of development, a state which requires different actions from collaborators at different moments.

In "Network Ecologies and Feminist Politics of 'Mass Sterilization' in Brazil," Rafael de la Dehesa, explores the concept of network ecologies within transnational feminism and describes it as an evolving constellation of public and private entities, circulating resources and knowledge. de la Dehesa argues that transnational network ecologies can cultivate solidarity while also being sites of confusion and misunderstanding, using the discourse around mass sterilization in Brazil as a case study. The work found here posits that interpretations of the Brazilian context misunderstood the situation and assumed governmental coercion into sterilization instead of inquiring about how women's agency was being demonstrated within a context with limited choices. Perhaps most beneficial for activist readers, is how de la Dehesa's extensive historical account demonstrates that network ecologies can develop in ways that create allies out of seemingly oppositional groups.

The midway point of *Transnational Feminist Itineraries*, chronologically but not ideologically, occurs in Part 3, "Interrogating Corporate Power," and begins with "Transnational Childhoods: Linking Global Production, Local Consumption, and Feminist Resistance" by Laura L. Lovett. "Transnational Childhoods" adds to conversations from anthropology which focus on childhood migration by acknowledging the power held by corporations and how their ability to determine available choices of children's products inherently limits demonstrations of agency on the part of children and parents alike. Due to an increasingly globalized market, engendered in part by legislation such as the North American Free Trade Agreement (NAFTA), corporations possess transnational influence over conceptions of gender roles and supposed norms. Lovett strategically argues that the global market, then, becomes a key site of interest for transnational feminism when considering the construction of the next generation's understanding of gender identity.

Concluding Part 3, Kathryn Moeller's "Nike's Search for Third World Potential: The Tensions between Corporate Funding and Feminist Futures" continues to interrogate ideas of who can just do transnational feminism. Moeller employs an ethnographic method to recount the experience of working on a transnational project. She explores how the educational program, which consisted of professional training for young women in poverty to enter sport-oriented workplaces, began with pre-imagined participants prior to entering local sites. The characteristics of participants then fit into a westernized, US-centric understanding of what the potential to end poverty meant. Moeller's account provides an accessible entry point for thinking through some of the difficulties involved with corporate sponsorship: the benefits of additional funding, recognition, and a proverbial seat at the table as well as some detriments such as the legitimization of corporate power, programs being structured to fit ever-changing corporate goals, and the framing of participants as resources or a means to an end, instead of being valuable in and of themselves.

The fourth section of *Transnational Feminist Itineraries*, "Intractable Dilemmas," opens with "Reproductive Justice and the Contradictions of International Surrogacy Claims by Gay Men in Australia" by Nancy A. Naples and Mary Bernstein. Chapter 9 focuses on the developing discourse around surrogacy, specifically in relation to Australia. Naples and Bernstein incorporate three sources of primary data within their NVivo coding: fifty-two interviews from legislators, activists, and people self-identifying as gay or lesbian, public statements from LGBTQ+ rights organizations, as well as articles published in various Australian newspapers (157–158). Curiously, Naples and Bernstein find that advocates of surrogacy outwardly supported transnational rather than domestic surrogacy. The co-authors prompt readers to consider the continuing line of colonialism within the outsourcing of surrogacy, citing Jyotsna A. Gupta who writes "that one's privileges in the world-system are always linked to another woman's oppression or exploitation" (169).

Part 4 closes with "Wombs in India: Revisiting Commercial Surrogacy" by Amrita Pande which seamlessly flows from the work of Naples and Bernstein who discuss at length the Australian use of surrogates from India. Pande, too, elaborates on the colonial nature of surrogacy, especially when clients frame their payment for services within a savior narrative, citing the assumed life change associated with the additional income. This narrative positions Indian women "not only as desperately poor but also as worthy poor" (185). The ability to label others as (not) deserving of a savior is enabled from the clients' position of power, in part engendered by the power associated with their respective nations, as well as issues of class, race, and religion as Pande discusses. Pande posits the need to not only acknowledge the agency of women opting to participate within commercial surrogacy, but to provide spaces for their voices to be heard and to make meaning *with* this community instead of having conversations *about* them.

Transnational Feminist Itineraries concludes with Part 5, Nationalisms and Plurinationalisms. This portion of the book begins with "Sporting Transnational Feminisms: Gender, Nation, and Women's Athletic Migrations between Brazil and the United States" by Cara K. Snyder, which focuses on how athletic teams and players participate in both the construction and critique of the imagined identities of nations. Snyder outlines how the movement of players between Brazil and the United States, predominantly to the US, created a space to discuss the ideological differences between the nations: an elevation of the importance of perceived femininity within a male-dominated soccer history and the centering of economic gain, respectively. Snyder does not include the voices of US-based players or coaches; however, the incorporation of (formerly) Brazilian athletes effectively demonstrates how "the unevenness of the global financial infrastructure" has positioned the US in a place of power, where its moves for capital gain have created a transnational perspective of the country as a sanctuary, as other discussions subordinate the financial one (199).

The penultimate chapter, of both the text and Part 5, "Mozambican Feminisms: Between the Local and the Global," by Isabel Maria Cortesão Casimiro and Catarina Casimiro Trindade demonstrate how the positioning of feminism as a "foreign intrusion" is used in places such as Mozambique to alienate the movement, disassociating it from the national identity (207). Chapter 12 discusses how individuals in power within the country have used tactics ranging from threats to kidnappings to the prohibition of feminist protests and public activities to maintain control and avoid critique. Feminism within Mozambique thus runs parallel to the US war on terror, creating a fear of outsiders while strengthening a particular communal identity and perception of sovereignty. "Mozambican Feminisms" challenges readers to engage in the necessary work of transnational feminism, while rendering the dangers inescapably palpable: as with accounts such as Jaime Macuane's, a political science professor, who was shot four times in the knees as a warning for his public critique of Mozambique's governance.

The closing chapter of *Transnational Feminist Itineraries,* "Plural Sovereignty and *la Familia Diversa* in Ecuador's 2008 Constitution" is a co-contributed piece written by Christine "Cricket" Keating and Amy Lind. Keating and Lind discuss the shifting language used within Ecuador's various constitutions and extensively map the contingent development of local feminist movements. Central to Chapter 13 is the dual exploration of the terms plurination and *la familia diversa,* or the diverse forms of families. Plurination is a term adopted within Ecuador's 2008 constitution that acknowledges the sovereignty of Indigenous and Afro-Ecuadorian groups as well as, as outlined by the Confederation of Indigenous Nationalities of Ecuador and presented by the authors, "denotes the process by which different autonomous groups can interact and coexist with respect and equality" (224). *La familia diversa* is a concept that recognizes and destigmatizes nonnormative family units and champions equal protections and affordances to them. The concluding chapter underlines that the value stemming from language changes within and across institutions originates in their use, a testing of what is permissible.

The introduction of *Transnational Feminist Itineraries* put forth the goal of furthering the development of feminist theories via a five-pronged approach, which I have delineated above. Varying success can be found in each of these areas. (1) The contributions create a compelling claim for the necessity of transnational feminist tools and methods within the current global context. (2) The parallels between intersectional and transnational feminisms are extensively illustrated; however, direct engagement with decolonial and post-colonial theories are limited, leaving the reader to parse out the relationship between the two. (3) Chapters within the text develop highly nuanced understandings of cross-border activism that map out transnational feminism's historical context. (4) Sections such as the introduction and Part 3 effectively demonstrate the value of both "scaling up" and "scaling out". (5) Two main critiques of transnational feminisms are briefly incorporated—the paradoxical focus on the US and the perceived elitism of language use. *Transnational Feminist Itineraries* effectively decenters the US within its discussion, however, the issue of language use largely goes unaddressed, perhaps due to the intended audience of the text. While written in a predominantly formal and academic register, various audiences would still find the discussions taking place within *Transnational Feminist Itineraries* both useful and approachable. The contributors successfully navigate the nuances between different feminisms, referring to relevant readings that provide established scholars, graduate students, and ambitious undergraduate students alike the ability to pursue further reading without requiring all readers to engage with the text in a formal academic way. The language within this text, while not being overtly theoretical, does build on styles of writing more common within academic spheres. The chapters are formatted via a combination of short subsections which allows readers to peruse the text quickly or in brief installments. Additionally, digestible explanations of theories—such as how post-colonial does not mean the impact of colonialism is no longer felt—do provide entry points for those who have not conducted extensive readings on each theory discussed (19). Whereas the language itself may be challenging at times, these compositional choices do welcome busy community organizers and activists to read the text at their own pace, between meetings, or wherever they can afford the time to spare, without feeling the need to devote hours at a time to engage with the text. That being said, this text may prove most useful to individuals and organizations who are either firmly established with self-sustaining networks, or those positioned near and actively working across the erected borders of nations. This is due in part to the continuous efforts and material resources that transnational feminist work requires.

Although the subtitle of the text, *Situating Theory and Activist Practice*, puts emphasis on activism, *Transnational Feminist Itineraries* does not focus on what much of this conversation means for activists today. The focus centers around the connection between activism and theory, situating it, but is not structured to serve as a "how-to" guide for readers. The text prioritizes and illustrates the historical context of transnational feminist activism via an assortment of case studies instead of generating tangible examples of what activism could look like, or providing suggestions for how to approach transnational work, beyond providing historical examples of what has been done. This may be in part due to the complexity of transnational feminist work. Offering potential suggestions or step-by-step guides is counterintuitive to a theory that recognizes the need for researchers and activists alike to situate themselves, to understand the investments of various stakeholders, and to recognize how these investments evolve over time within each individual context. Offering a checklist of how to conduct transnational feminist work risks flattening the identities of academics, activists, and communities alike. It would assume sameness instead of cultivating solidarity.

Readers of *Community Literacy Journal* may find this text useful even if they do not currently engage in transnational work. While each chapter offers insight into methods for collaboration, the introduction and sections on scale may be points of particular interest as they directly address how collaboration is possible amongst dissenting constituencies. Working with communities necessarily entails working with individuals who hold varying viewpoints and thinking about how to bridge those differences to create solidarity. This edited collection may also be useful for those working within larger cities, which generally host diverse populations. Those within towns with agriculturally based economic systems may also find this text helpful in considering the transnational flow of labor and capital in connection with food production, as many workers traverse national borders in the pursuit of work. Community literacy workers within the US will recognize the increasingly divisive socio-political context, as well as the increasing diversity of the communities within which we work. In sum, *Transnational Feminist Itineraries* provides in-depth analyses of how borders, whether geographical or ideological, do not need to be barriers to collaborative action.

Words No Bars Can Hold: Literacy Learning in Prison

Deborah Appleman
W.W. Norton and Company, 2019, pp.160

Reviewed by Walter Lucken IV
Wayne State University

In my time facilitating a creative writing workshop at a state prison outside Detroit, I have often questioned the function of my work. Especially given my own commitments to abolitionist politics, the precis of my late-night ponderings is essentially the extent to which I and my work function as an extension of the carceral state. I don't expect to find a hard and fast answer, and I suspect that if I did it would be something along the lines of "both/and." However, I will say for certain that I was glad to see Deborah Appleman interrogate the "what for" of prison literacy education in her recent monograph *Words No Bars Can Hold: Literacy Learning in Prison*.

Appleman's book takes as its central conceit the notion that the traditional value afforded to a liberal arts education, rather than being inappropriate for incarcerated writers, can in fact find its truest form amongst incarcerated students. In the first chapter, which doubles as the introduction, Appleman sets up this proposal by noting that vocational programs in prisons are much easier to make a case for than liberal arts education or arts programming, in that they prepare returning citizens for gainful employment, often in skilled trades positions. Liberal arts education and arts programming, on the other hand, have little demonstrable value in economic terms. One can make a case that these programs lower recidivism and support incarcerated students in learning the skills and dispositions appropriate for their life after release, and indeed I and many others do. The fatal flaw in this argument, however, is that it leaves out those incarcerated for life, who ostensibly will never leave prison, a not insignificant portion of the incarcerated. For these prospective students, any education they undertake will only benefit them in the context of their lives in prison, leaving few avenues for argumentation in the favor of such an enterprise, at least in the current *doxa*.

Indeed, the value of a liberal arts education has been in question for decades in the United States, including for "traditional" students, even those who enjoy the most privilege. For Appleman and myself, then, this places us in the position of arguing that our society should afford a privilege to its most maligned members which it is increasingly unwilling to grant to its most valued young people. Appleman takes up this challenge with courage and resolve in the following chapters, arguing that to make a case for the value of liberal arts education and literacy learning for those serving life sentences is to make a case for its value writ large, in that the incarcerated are the only students in a position to seek the true benefits of education for their own sake, as their circumstances obviate the potential for education to be used as a means to any end other than itself.

The second chapter details the environment in which Appleman's prison courses take place, a scene which any prison educator will find immediately familiar. This is to say that Appleman is masterful in her narration of the experience of entering the physical world of the incarcerated as a person who otherwise spends most of their time in the academic environment, and how the experience of physically entering and teaching in prison frames the entire experience. I found this to be the case myself, in that learning how to manage the anxiety I felt in the carceral environment was my greatest challenge at first, much more than managing the workshop itself or even building relationships with my co-participants. In short, Appleman notes that simply being in the prison is sometimes the most important lesson, and to an extent an important precondition for truly understanding the importance of prison education.

The second chapter explores the contradictions of liberal arts learning and critical pedagogy in a carceral environment, and how those contradictions can serve as a helpful opportunity to rethink the ways that we've understood the liberating role of education historically. Beginning with an anecdote in which a student recounts to Appleman how her pedagogical choices reflect, in his estimation, the values professed by Paulo Freire, the chapter goes on to engage the notion that liberal arts education is particularly helpful for incarcerated students insofar as it can assist them in reframing their personal narratives. This is to say that with the new vistas that literacy learning affords them, incarcerated students can begin to understand their self-concept in terms beyond the choices that led them to prison or even the circumstances which fomented those choices. In short, Appleman argues that education as the development of "intelligence plus character", as Martin Luther King Jr. puts it, is not only particularly appropriate, but vital to incarcerated learners.

Next, in "No Hugs for Thugs", Appleman explores how the logics of surveillance and control which underpin the carceral environment present serious impediments to the cultivation of genuine relationships between prison educators and their students, that is, the relationships which many of us rely on as the ultimate condition of possibility for any genuine learning to take place. This chapter particularly resonated with me as well, in that I too do my work in a facility in which any physical contact beyond a handshake is expressly forbidden, and a state in which I am to have no contact with any inmate in the Michigan Department of Corrections for the entirety of my time as a registered volunteer. Thus, throughout the COVID-19 pandemic, I have relied on secondhand communication for any update on how my collaborators are doing and had extremely limited opportunities to solicit input from them while engaged in the editing and publishing of their work. I know well the dilemmas Appleman recounts in the chapter, and I found this chapter to get closer to the narrative unconscious that I either perceived or projected while working my way through the chapters: abolition. This is to say that, in this chapter especially, but throughout the rest of the book as well, Appleman's account of her experiences points to the carceral state as a major obstruction to human flourishing and development in the contemporary United States. Thus, to me, Appleman's book underscores that the modern prison system functions as an impediment to the normative goals and commitments of all educators, whether they directly work inside prisons or not.

The next chapter considers the concrete role of literacy education and related enterprises in supporting incarcerated writers in their efforts to be granted parole, seek their own release, ask for re-sentencing, and so on. At the risk of repeating myself, this too was a familiar story for me. As I write this review, the prosecutor's office in Michigan's most populous county (which includes Detroit) continues to stall the re-sentencing of more than one hundred people, mostly men, who were sentenced to life as juveniles prior to such sentences being declared unconstitutional by 2012's Miller v. Alabama decision in the United States Supreme Court. This cohort includes a few of my collaborators, namely Yusuf Qualls-El and Stephen Hibbler, the latter of which maintains his innocence. Thus, the role of prison literacy education as a vehicle for students to literally "write their way out of prison", as the chapter's title puts it, is underscored by the extent to which this is a primary objective for many students.

The next chapter, which includes a few beautiful selections of poetry from Appleman's students, considers the role of literacy in helping these incarcerated writers manage their mental health, specifically from the perspective of the state's legal obligations to those it incarcerates. This would likely be a controversial argument if only for the fact that, as noted above, the so-called privileges this scenario would extend to incarcerate people are indeed privileges which our society currently declines to afford universally. Appleman seems to imply, and I will state explicitly, that in fact guaranteeing such rights to the incarcerated can be a vehicle for making a case for the extension of those rights to all, particularly in a society which incarcerates people at the rate that the United States does.

The next chapter examines the relationships that Appleman's students had to schools and education prior to coming to prison, and how in many ways the attitudes and structures of the public school system can fail young people and contribute to their later incarceration. Taking the commonplace notion of the "school to prison pipeline" as her point of departure alongside her simultaneous roles teaching in a public high school as well as the prison, she narrates how she finds herself wondering how many of the young men and women who slip through the cracks of the education system will ultimately end up in prison, and how early interventions in public school students' lives might help them avoid later incarceration. While in earlier chapters I sometimes found myself wondering how Appleman's arguments might be augmented with an abolitionist intervention, it was this chapter where I found myself being most critical, in that Appleman narrates how the benefits of literacy education might prevent incarceration as well as reduce the violence of incarceration, or in rare cases end it for an individual. When we move to the structural level though, it is important to recognize that mass incarceration is the result of an explicit and intentional decision on the part of the United States to utilize incarceration as a means of resolving social problems, as opposed to the outcome of failures in other social systems.

The final chapter includes a few more stunning pieces of writing by Appleman's students and ends on the note that if we are going to keep people in prisons, we must keep them human. In this way, Appleman connects back to her earlier claim, that liberal arts education, rather than being inappropriate for the carceral environment, indeed finds its fullest expression in such a context. Thus, Appleman's ultimate claim is that to incarcerate people without offering them access to the things that make them human in fact runs counter to the normative purpose of incarceration, which is of course rehabilitating incarcerated people and supporting their transition into society upon their release. In this sense, Appleman continues her earlier line of argumentation wherein liberal arts education not only finds its fullest expression in the carceral context but is also vital for the well being of those who reside there, skillfully coming full circle in the transition to the epilogue.

Appleman ends by recounting the recent murder of a corrections officer by an incarcerated person in the facility where she teaches, illuminating another ever-present aspect of prison literacy education, one which we must in some ways ignore to go on about our work. Namely, the unending cycles of violence and brutality which permeate the carceral system. In a sense, this is an especially sobering point to end on, which I for one appreciate. The fact is that the victories and accomplishments we relish so much in prison literacy education are made even more meaningful by the greater context of despair and injustice which surrounds them, which sadly means that the unjust nature of the carceral system is in many ways the condition of possibility for the work which we find so meaningful.

In *Words No Bars Can Hold*, I found a great deal of helpful reflection and insight about prison literacy education, not only by recognizing this work in my own experiences but also seeing the ways in which Appleman's courses and students are different from my own. Prison educators, a small but meaningful community, will greatly benefit from Appleman's book and its courageous efforts to sift through the contradictions of literacy teaching in prison. Advocates for prison reform and abolition who do not teach in prisons will also find important insight here, most notably how incarceration curtails and forecloses on many of the values we hold most important. Also, anyone concerned with literacy education, liberal arts education, and the arts will find Appleman's book to be of great import, not least because of the current emphasis on criminal justice reform and abolitionist politics in those realms, but because Appleman's thoughts have great importance for the future of literacy learning writ large in the twenty-first century.

In this review, I have critiqued *Words No Bars Can Hold* for not going further in its analysis of the purpose of incarceration. Put simply, I suggest that to fully realize the promise of the book, we need to go beyond the liberal reformist framework that Appleman ultimately remains within. This is not to say that I do not understand possible reasons for doing so; I certainly exercise great caution in how I make certain arguments in certain contexts as well, for reasons Appleman makes clear. Namely, the potential consequences for our missteps as prison educators are always most acutely experienced by our incarcerated students and collaborators. In closing, I merely suggest that the costs of waiting for the right moment are now greater than the costs of stepping toward the abolitionist horizon, both in and out of prison literacy classrooms.

Queer Literacies: Discourses and Discontents

Mark McBeth
Lexington Books, 2019, pp. 271

Reviewed by Mary F. McGinnis
College of Coastal Georgia

Mark McBeth's *Queer Literacies: Discourses and Discontents* uses his own Queer literacy narrative ("auto-archival self-investigation") and Queer ethnographic artifacts created by others ("books, archives, memoirs, and other memory banks") to frame an explication of how the rhetoric surrounding queerness has changed since the homophile movement of the early twentieth century (6). These techniques encourage readers to identify with him and the Queer activists he discusses. This book would be an excellent resource for scholars and advanced graduate students interested in rhetoric, (auto)ethnographic research, literacy, pedagogy, Queer history, and Queer theory. The overarching goal of the text is to emphasize the purpose Queer literates, that is Queer rhetors who "practiced discursive performativity that made words do things that would transform the world in which they lived," served in combatting the homophobic and heterosexist practices and messages put forth by various types of publications and institutions (3). Barbara Gittings is heavily featured as a key Queer literate activist and agent of change. Each chapter of the text focuses on a different cultural institution and examines the part that institution played in shaping the discourse on Queer lives historically and today. The book has *kairos* in that the Queer literate's job is never done—learning from the past and seeing the strategies Queer literates used to move public opinion about Queer people will be useful to today's Queer literates.

In Chapter 1, "Queer Literacies on the Brain," McBeth situates his theorizing by starting at the beginning—the beginning of his own Queer literacy journey and at the beginning of the Queer movement. He discloses that as a young Queer person in a heterosexist world, he had to conceptualize and reconceptualize his world and worldview to create a place where he fit in; he pairs these experiences with the reality of the archived experiences of other LGBTQ people. Building upon this structure, the author takes these first-hand experiences a step further to clarify "how literacy sponsorships played a role in the dynamic power play between heteronormative/homophobic public discourses and Queer subject formation in common place public venues such as family dinner tables, doctor's offices, bible schools, and elementary classrooms, or other public forums" (9). Using Deborah Brandt's definition of literacy sponsors, that is "figures who turned up most typically in people's memories of literacy learning" (e.g. relatives, teachers, clergy, writers, etc.) in conjunction with Michael Warner's theories of publics and counter-publics, McBeth illuminates the ways that "literacy sponsorships and their underlying platforms shaped homosexuality as a discursively 'objective' subject; and then subsequent Queer counter-literacy measures reclaimed a discursive foothold to reinvent their subjective public image(s)" (9, 14, 28). McBeth successfully creates a framework to examine "literacy normalcy," how Queer rhetors are shaped by literacy sponsorships, and, in turn, how these Queer rhetors reshape the publics around them.

Chapter 2, "Archival Tracks and Traces: Evidence of Queer Literacies," highlights the importance of literacy to Queer lives and accentuates the ways that literacy has allowed Queer literates to resist and work against heteronormative discourses and hegemonies. McBeth begins the chapter by sharing a portion of Barbara Gittings' literacy recollections:

> I flunked out of college as the end of my freshman year because I had stopped going to classes in order to run around to libraries and spend my time reading about myself in categories such as "Sexual Perversions"—and wondering and worrying. When I returned home in disgrace, I couldn't explain to my parents what was wrong, and I still knew no one I could approach to talk to—so back to the stacks I went. (35)

This narrative will resonate with many pre-internet Queer people—McBeth uses it to reinforce the important place literacy played in the self-definition of Queer literates and to show the double-edged sword that literacy presented. Queer people used all available means to discover themselves, but much of the literature available was created by heteronormative/homophobic literacy sponsorships, sharing inaccurate and damaging information, often with young and vulnerable people. McBeth builds on Gittings' narrative, sharing brief vignettes that showcase his own journey of self-discovery as a Queer person as well as stories from Queer activists, like Judith Grahn, Harry Hay, and Fenton Johnson. These narratives further solidify the important functions that literacy, reading, and text play in the lives and self-discovery of Queer people. McBeth points out that Queer literacy gave people the chance to resist heteronormative cultural narratives and to "expose the misinformation and false claims" that "the established and accepted literacy authorities" made about Queer people (54). Experiences like the ones described in this chapter fueled Queer literates to fact-check texts, disseminate unbiased research, and rewrite literature on homosexuality to accurately reflect Queer lives as normal and healthy.

Shifting focus in Chapter 3, "Adult Supervision: Insights to Queer Silence, *or* Family Got Your Tongue?," the author reviews the history and evolution of Parents and Friends of Lesbians and Gays (PFLAG), detailing the role the organization played in literacy efforts to shift the rhetoric surrounding Queer people. Citing Catherine Tuerk, McBeth highlights that PFLAG literature was some of the first material she was exposed to that didn't "make [her] think that being gay was *disgusting, sick, or sinful*" (80). Further, McBeth presents Tuerk's experiences to "underscore the reparative literacy labors that happened among PFLAG members and that constantly rerouted them to new research and effective ways to recirculate this knowledge" (81). The work done by PFLAG since its inception in 1973 is evidence that "literacy-laden and love-based activism can shift cultural discourses" (86). McBeth explains how PFLAG confronts anti-LGBTQ ideologies and thwarts heteronormative discourse.

Chapter 4, "Teacher Teacher: Queer Literacies in K-16" discusses the gendered socialization taught in school and how teachers were charged with "reproducing normative behavior and rehabilitating those that undermined socially accepted norms" (99). He begins the chapter by recounting a story of his elementary school teacher gender policing his eleven-year old self. She disapproves of him playing with the girls at recess:

> . . . she called out, "Mark McBeth, will you come to the front of the room please?" Not knowing her intentions and with the confidence of a designated [high-performing smart] child, I approached the front of the classroom. . . She prompted me "I'd like you to tell the class why you prefer to play with girls, and then explain to them, why you're not proud of your masculinity?" While I stared at her and my classmates stared at me, their silence anticipating my yet-unspoken words, our silence in deference to the now ominously quiet teacher, her silence pursed and impatient for an answer. . . Beyond the burning blush that I felt in front of my peers. . . I must honestly say that I don't remember how else I felt. . . I knew that crying in front of my classmates would have only justified her accusation, guilty as charged, a sentence of sissy guilt. (93)

He uses this and another experience as a launch pad to dive into the pedagogical education teacher trainees received in the 1930s through examining teacher training textbooks. He reveals that teachers, steeped in eugenics and biological essentialism, were to "act as educational vigilantes, staying alert to defects and abnormalities that they should then attempt to rectify" in an effort to "improve the race" (104). Drawing his examination forward to the 1970s, McBeth shares the "Bill of Rights for Gay Teachers and Students" from the New York Gay Teachers Association and the Columbia Student Homophile League's "Statement of Purpose" to illustrate the action that Queer literates took to enact "official institutional protocols" to change education and confront institutional homophobia within the education system (112–121). This chapter showcases direct actions that Queer literates used to reform treatment of LGBTQ people in the educational sphere.

In Chapter 5, "'Gay books? Libraries? That Rang Bells for me!': Reforming the Literacy Platforms," the author returns to Barbara Gittings' activism with the Gay Task Force of the American Library Association. The chapter reiterates her efforts to "shift heteronormative platforms of library policy and practice" and replace them with "literate sponsorships in which Queer literates could find accurate facts and empowering words" (132, 133). Recounting Gittings' work alongside other librarians, McBeth explains the steps they took to include LGBTQ acquisitions in the library, resist "the heteronormative cycle of deaccessioning Gay materials," and surveying encyclopedia entries to ensure they provided "unbiased and objective information on homosexuality and *healthy* Lesbian or Gay sensibilities" (145, 161, 166). The contributions and importance of Gittings' activism is reiterated in this chapter and links back to the discussion of the importance of libraries and literacy in Queer self-discovery from Chapter 1.

Focusing on scientific texts and their depictions of homosexuality, Chapter 6, "Psycho-Babble: Literacies as Dangers and Salvations," McBeth opens the chapter by recounting his exploration of the term "homosexuality" in the *Modern Home Medical Advisor*, a medical encyclopedia published from 1935 to 1969 (174). Early editions of the text had "homosexuality" listed; however, later editor, Morris Fishbein, buried any mention of homosexuality under "the Crush," relegating it to young girls' deep friendships and urging that the crush "should not be allowed to develop to an intimacy which approaches a homosexual level" (176). McBeth critiques Fishbein, stating "Any scholarly rhetoric has been omitted [from *Modern Home Medical Advisor*] and replaced with subjective opinion, impersonating social edict" (176). In this chapter, McBeth presents evidence from "a group of psychiatric 'authorities' on homosexuality," finding that "the medical rhetoric for Queers between 1930 and 1980 shifted from various levels of denial of existence, to a mishap of heredity, to a case for criminal lunacy, to a target for psychotherapy, to an experiment in conversion therapy" and more that continues to today (177). Once he presents this evidence, he explains how Queer literates worked to change this medical discourse. For example, Frank Kameny's critiques of the psychiatric community and work with Barbara Gittings, lobbying the APA to remove "homosexuality" from the Diagnostic and Statistical Manual of Mental Disorders (DSM) and Jay Prosser's later efforts to remove "transsexualism" from the DSM (190–193, 197). Queer literates are still working to change the rhetoric of the medical community toward LGBTQ people.

Moving forward to the 1980s, Chapter 7, "Viral Impetus: The Rhetorical-Literate Activism of ACT UP," is notably much shorter than the other chapters in the text. The author remarks that this is to "point to the abbreviated lives that People with AIDS" had during that time period, adding that "an incredible brain trust of Queer literates was lost in the twentieth century... and we should not forget how the literacy lives of Queer literates lost helped in the efforts to act up, fight back, fight AIDS" (126–127). This chapter sets the scene for governmental dismissal of the AIDS crisis and focuses on the rhetorical action taken by ACT UP, both publicly and "behind-the-desk," to raise awareness of the crisis and to "uncover the unwieldy practices and discriminating policies of power-wielding organizations overseen by governmental agencies, pharmaceutical corporations, insurance companies, and medical conglomerates" (214). This chapter illustrates the literal life-or-death struggle Queer literates faced in the fight against AIDS and the way AIDS was presented in the public sphere.

In Chapter 8, "In Conclusion, Queer Literacy's Inconclusiveness," McBeth ends the text with the assertion that "Queer literacy has not concluded" because "as sponsors of homophobia/heteronormativity continue to rework their discursive powers, into more elaborate, nuanced, yet no less vicious rhetorical arguments, so do Queer literates need to polish their pearls of rhetorical wisdom" (231). He recaps how society has changed, the actions Queer literates have taken, and attempts to smooth over the "divide between activist and academic" Queer literates (237). In his smoothing, he refers readers back to the archives to hear and tell "the stories of others to confirm, complicate, and contest our narratives, so the telling can remain queer, so it doesn't become normativized" (239). This chapter maintains that while Queer literates have accomplished much, the work is not complete. As heteronormative forces shift their attacks on Queer lives, it is important to remain vigilant and continue using literacy to support an accurate and empowering Queer rhetoric.

This book is a helpful resource full of many examples of cultural criticism and rhetorical analysis of cultural texts. It provides a literacy-focused review of LGBTQ history and how Queer literates shifted the current cultural climate. This text would be useful as a textbook for a graduate-level rhetoric course to provide examples of how to complete ethnographic case studies. The personal stories and pieces from archives make the book interesting and engaging.

Literacy Heroines: Women and the Written Word

Alice S. Horning
Peter Lang Publishing, 2021, pp. 303

Reviewed by Andrea McCrary
Queens University of Charlotte

Early in my career at the small comprehensive university founded on the liberal arts where I work, I was fortunate to teach in an innovative interdisciplinary program and was regularly supported by the senior faculty members with whom I taught. One such mentor was an experienced faculty member in the History Department who reminded me that much of the value of studying stories of those who have come before us lies in the consideration of the "past that is present." Drawing connections between the stories of the past and the struggles of the present is, in fact, what many of us do in our classrooms. In *Literacy Heroines: Women and the Written Word,* Alice S. Horning takes this approach, presenting the work of twelve notable women from the Modern period of 1880–1930, drawing significance from both their activities in their own contexts and from the models they offer those of us concerned about key issues facing our contemporary communities. As such, Horning offers readers a text that both satisfies as a work of literacy history and challenges us to see how the strategies used by these women may serve the scholars, writers, and activists seeking change today.

The introduction of the book presents Horning's rationale for collecting the stories of these women and arranging the chapters as she does. Before her comments on the identities and roles of the women, she begins with some key definitions, establishing shared understanding of "literacy" and "modernity" as a foundation for discussing the work of these women. Here, she highlights the similarities between the modern period and today, specifically indicating the significance of "intense change" including "demographic shifts" and "huge waves of immigration"—all of which are obviously resonant for a contemporary reader (6). Moving to a definition of "intersectionality," Horning asserts that the "concept makes a great deal of sense when looking at the work of the heroines. . . . [given that] their approach inevitably entailed underlying intersections of gender, race, class, ethnicity or other factors" (12). Indeed, each chapter aims to acknowledge and consider the various ways intersectional identities affect the work of each woman. Further, the introduction establishes definitions for three central designations that she uses for each of the women: Exemplar/

Expert, Sponsor, and Literacy Heroine. Exemplars, Horning notes, demonstrate skill and credentials, but "experts also need experience in their chosen field" to fulfill the expectations of the role (14). Sponsors demonstrate the value of literacy by "sharing their knowledge and expertise" (14). Finally, as Horning shapes the definition of the title phrase, "Literacy Heroine," she homes in on the lens through which she sees the women whose stories are collected in the book: she states that "a literacy heroine is a woman who has worked in a variety of roles, using her literacy abilities in heroic efforts to serve as a respected exemplar/expert and sponsor of literacy for others" (17). In providing these definitions, Horning highlights the selection of these women as literacy heroines in their own historical contexts and their relevance to the issues facing contemporary communities that may draw from their examples.

In this way, Horning has set out to write a book focused on women "whose work on literacy made substantial difference in the lives of others" (52). The methodology, essentially a case study approach, finds Horning reviewing not only primary work written by each woman, but also critical work by other writers, including biographers and journalists. Notably, Horning draws from interviews with contemporary scholars who have knowledge of these women, and she reports following the feminist practice of sharing the completed work with those interview subjects as a means of ensuring accuracy in her portrayal of their ideas. The introduction to the book, then, reinforces Horning's careful process in gathering and presenting the work of these extraordinary women writers.

Following the introduction, the book presents the stories of a dozen women, arranging their chapters around the arenas in which Horning sees their most notable work: education, activism, and writing. The women included as educators are Mary McLeod Bethune, Gertrude Buck, Cora Wilson Stewart, and Sarah Winnemucca. Horning includes Jane Addams, Mary Church Terrell, Lilian Wald, and Ida B. Wells-Barnett in the activist section. Finally, the women in the section on writers are Nella Larsen, Josephine St. Pierre Ruffin, Harriet Beecher Stowe, and Ida Tarbell. Many of the women included in *Literacy Heroines* are well-known to students and scholars of the late-19th and early 20th century social movements, though some will be new. The structure of the book allows readers to take in the dozen stories in various ways—as a whole, as a group in one of the three main sections, or as individual chapters that can stand alone for readers interested in singular cases. Additionally, while Horning focuses her attention narrowly on the work of women in using literacy to confront social ills, the breadth of identities related to class, race, and ethnicity provides a broad sense of the relevant issues and effects of the work done by these women in the Modern period.

Rather than provide details from each chapter, as each woman's story provides myriad significant moments (more than this review can hold), I want to highlight Horning's arrangement and approach, as they offer important revelations for readers. By grouping these women according to activity—Educators, Activists, and Writers—Horning highlights the limits on women's lives in the Modern period while also demonstrating the possibilities for confronting societal problems from within those limits. Within these sections, the arrangement of each chapter provides a consistent lens through which to view the women's contributions to literacy in their communities. Horning has crafted a tight structure, creating clarity, accessibility, and a clear through line for the discussion.

Each chapter begins with a brief introduction before moving into a context-setting "Issue of the Times" section in which Horning situates the women according to the prevalent events and issues in their communities. These issues are far ranging, but all significant; they include specific legal moments like the *Plessy v Ferguson* decision or the Dawes Act, as well as broader movements on issues of racism, suffrage, immigration, labor, and indigenous rights. In each chapter, this section highlights the issue most relevant to the woman being discussed. Next, each chapter moves to a biographical sketch of the woman, emphasizing elements of each woman's life that seem most relevant to their work in the communities. Specifically, Horning here turns to relational details like family background and connections to other people doing similar work, along with educational background and achievements. Here, Horning often points out the important sponsors in these women's lives, further underscoring the importance of literacy sponsors in the development of literacy heroines.

Following the background sections in each chapter, Horning discusses each woman as they fulfill the significant roles of exemplar, sponsor, and heroine defined in the introduction. In enumerating the achievements of these women, Horning highlights the breadth of their accomplishments offering readers a glimpse into the remarkable achievements of these women. The book includes women who founded or led educational institutions (i.e., Bethune, Stewart, and Buck) as well as women who founded or led social organizations (i.e., Addams, Terrell, and Ruffin). Despite the notable diversity of experience and focus represented by these women, the noteworthy commonality as Horning presents them is their achievement in writing; writing dissertations and novels or essays, speeches, and columns, these women uniformly represent the power of literacy to speak to and against the social concerns of the writer and her allies. In pointing out the written work as well as the organizational and leadership work that these women represent, Horning reinforces her thesis that these women achieved the accomplishments they did largely through their successful deployment of literacy work.

Just before a list of references related to the heroine in each chapter, readers will find a section headed "Lessons for Contemporary Times" in which Horning calls attention to the attribute that best served each woman in her work. Having pointed to research on grit as a foundational idea, she regularly highlights the persistence that propelled the women through the challenges they faced, often as a result of their intersectional identities. While these women certainly demonstrated resilience in a world that resisted them and their work, I struggled a bit with the repeated reliance on grit as a defining characteristic. However, I found the inclusion of qualities like Terrell's networking and encouragement of coordination among women more useful, as this kind of collective approach serves as an important model for how women may face contemporary challenges in their communities. Indeed, bookending each chapter with "Issues of the Times" and "Lessons for Contemporary Times" provides readers a way of seeing how the past is present with us. In this way, Horning highlights both the challenges and the mechanisms of change available to these literacy heroines. While such a tight structure could be seen as repetitive or rigid, some students, particularly undergraduates, will likely find the pattern helpful in realizing the ways these diverse women resisted the challenges of their times in various ways, all with a sense of progress and vision.

Horning's final chapter, "Lessons and Conclusions," brings the significance of the work of these women into sharper relief with "an imagined opportunity for the heroines to make clear the lessons we might learn from the work that they did" (271). While each of the chapters focuses on one woman's work, this final chapter draws the work of the women together in a sense to reflect how their work responded to challenges of health and wellness, education, intellectual development, governmental regulation, citizenship, and racism. Recognizing the ways that these issues shaped the work of the heroines, Horning reminds readers that the lessons of the past really do have a place in our work today in that these issues represent ongoing struggles in the contemporary world. Strikingly, she includes in the final chapter comments from scholars whose work informs the view of the heroines that she constructs and a brief acknowledgement that to choose a dozen remarkable women requires the omission of others. She concedes that "while there might be another book to be written about both women and men overlooked here, they are kindly set aside to allow the Heroines to come to the fore" (285). I appreciate the recognition and the challenge that other stories remain to be written.

While Horning's discussion of how issues are met in complex contexts could have also included more acknowledgement of systemic change, the individual activities and collaborative approaches Horning's heroines undertake offer important examples to students of history, social change, literacy education, and writing to consider. I appreciate Horning's work in highlighting the strengths and weaknesses of these women, as well as her inclusion of multiple voices on their work. While each chapter provides only a brief overview of the tremendous labor undertaken by the woman of focus, the chapters can stand alone as useful introductions to women whose work may be new to students, with useful lists of references to guide further study. Importantly, though, reading the book as a whole provides further evidence that women have been doing the heroic work of "addressing the many forms of inequality in American society; their lives and work show that literacy is thus a key tool in the struggle for social justice, then and now" (291). In providing us with such an overview of these women, after other significant writing in the field, Horning takes her place among them, as this work of feminist history situates her as both exemplar and sponsor herself. I hope that we all continue to learn from the stories of these women whose work precedes us and continue to uncover the long trails of influence in the work of the contemporary literacy heroines among us.

www.ingramcontent.com/pod-product-compliance
Lightning Source LLC
Chambersburg PA
CBHW031347160426
43196CB00007B/754